ABOUT THE AUTHOR

S. DANA HUBBARD, M.D., (1869–1937) was director of the New York City Department of Health's Bureau of Public Health Education during the 1920s.

ABOUT THE EDITORS

BOB BERKOWITZ and SUSAN YAGER-BERKOWITZ are the authors of *Why Men Stop Having Sex: Men, the Phenomenon of Sexless Relationships, and What You Can Do About It.* Dr. Bob Berkowitz has a Ph.D. in clinical sexology. He is the author of the bestselling *What Men Won't Tell You but Women Need to Know.* A veteran reporter, he has been the men's correspondent on NBC's *Today* show and the host of *Real Personal* on CNBC. Susan Yager-Berkowitz is a long-time magazine writer, specializing in nutrition. Together Bob and Susan are the "Marriage Experts" on ThirdAge.com. They live on the east end of Long Island and in New York City.

DR. HUBBARD'S

SEX FACTS

for

MEN AND WOMEN

HARPER

NEW YORK • LONDON • TORONTO • SYDNEY

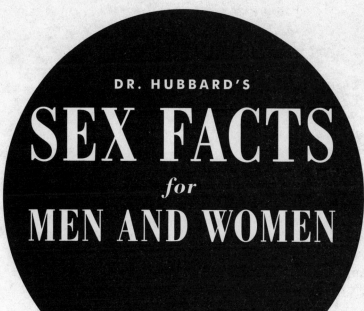

DR. HUBBARD'S

SEX FACTS

for

MEN AND WOMEN

S. DANA HUBBARD, M.D.

Edited by

BOB BERKOWITZ AND SUSAN YAGER-BERKOWITZ

HARPER

HarperCollins books may be purchased for educational, business, or sales promotional use. For information please write: Special Markets Department, HarperCollins Publishers, 10 East 53rd Street, New York, NY 10022.

FIRST EDITION

Designed by Justin Dodd

Library of Congress Cataloging-in-Publication Data is available upon request.

ISBN 978-0-06-170255-6

09 10 11 12 13   OV/RRD   10 9 8 7 6 5 4 3 2 1

CONTENTS

EDITORS' INTRODUCTION

Women born after the turn of the twentieth century were twice as likely to have lost their virginity prior to marriage as women of the previous generation. Indeed, America was rapidly changing in many ways when S. Dana Hubbard, in his impassioned, priggish attempt to "throw light where shadows fall," wrote this series of pamphlets in 1922. *Too fast*, a lot of people, including Dr. Hubbard, would probably have said, while simultaneously acknowledging that *some* new things—automobiles and motion pictures, for example—were wonderful.

It was a time of contradictions. When World War I ended in 1918, many young men returned from "over there" with a heightened level of sexual sophistication, having come in contact with European prostitutes—and syphilis and gonorrhea. Condom distribution had unwisely been prohibited. Meanwhile, the Eighteenth Amendment, ratified in 1919, was supposed to end the drinking problem. The following year, the Nineteenth Amendment gave women the right to vote, later than some Western countries but twenty-five years before France and fifty years before Switzerland.

Women were becoming empowered in other ways, too. Many did all the things we've come to associate with the "Roaring Twenties"—bob their hair, drink gin, smoke in public, listen to jazz, and Charleston all night. Young women known as "flappers," because of their breezy style of wearing unbuckled galoshes, symbolized the feminist movement. As one writer put it: "The real reason for the flapper's cigarette, the inciting cause of her pocket flask, the motive that lurks behind her petting parties, is her assertion that now she has become man's equal—and as such has a right to the sins he's been 20,000 years accumulating."[1]

Petting parties! Pocket flasks! Things seemed out of control to Samuel Dana Hubbard, Presbyterian and Freemason. Born in Montgomery, Alabama, in 1869, Hubbard received his M.D. from Bellevue Hospital Medical College in New York City, where he set up private practice and served as dermatologist at a children's hospital. He was affiliated with the New York City Department of Health for more than forty years, primarily as director of the Bureau of Public Health Education. In that time, he would wage a war against what he considered to be a lack of discretion and "overindulgence."

---

1 Lowry, Helen Bullitt. "From Flapper to Girl Scout." *New York Times*. October 23, 1921.

Hubbard was a conservative but unorthodox thinker, and it was this independence that likely led him to attorney and film distributor Samuel Cummins, who specialized in sensationalistic media. Cummins's "exploitation" films, advertised on the inside and back cover of every pamphlet, represent one of America's earliest examples of cross-marketing to a targeted audience.

The entrepreneurial Cummins likely presented Hubbard with an idea that was sure to appeal to him: In this world where decent men, women, and children's lives were being destroyed by venereal diseases and out-of-wedlock pregnancies, let's use the far-reaching power of direct selling and mail order to educate people of all ages about the terrible consequences of illicit passion. Teach them the "Facts of Life." The doctor would write, and Cummins would get the material published and distributed. Printed words would reinforce motion pictures. Hubbard had already acted as adviser on Cummins's 1919 film *Some Wild Oats*, which was loosely based on an early-twentieth-century French play about the horrors of venereal disease. Although most of the medical community was beginning to distance itself from films dedicated to "hygienic causes" (by 1927 the *Journal of Social Hygiene* called people associated with them "charlatans"[2]), Hubbard would continue to collaborate with Cummins for the rest of his life.

---

2 Schaefer, Eric. (1999) *Bold! Daring! Shocking! True! A History of Exploitation Films, 1919–1959*. Durham and London, Duke University Press, p. 37.

SEX ADVICE WITHOUT SEX

If people bought the original pamphlets hoping to get their hands on something salacious, or even to genuinely learn about sex, they were probably disappointed. The one thing never discussed is the sex act. In "Sex Facts for Young Men," an anatomical drawing of the male body omits the penis. However, Hubbard delivers a vivid clinical description, informing readers that the penis consists of "erectile tissue arranged in three cylindrical compartments—like a two barreled shot gun with its ramrod underneath."

Surely the reason most people paid a dollar for this series (the equivalent of about thirteen dollars today) was the pamphlet that promised "Facts About Marriage Every Young Man & Woman Should Know." At last, a young woman who doesn't know much can learn what to expect when she's expecting to have sex for the first time in her life. Imagine her anxiously turning the pages to find only: "There is a definite physical side to marriage." But, she may wonder, what in the world does that mean? What happens on the wedding night? Hubbard tells her: "Have a confidential talk with your parents, especially your mother or some other married woman, about the obligations of the marriage relation as it affects the wife or mother." That was it. The conversation was over, except to stress chastity during the engagement period. She should also "be sure the marriage license is legal" and "the person performing the ceremony is duly authorized," because girls can be "victimized" by "fake" marriages. Some frightened young women probably believed every word, but one can also imagine flappers laughing until their galoshes fell off.

Hubbard is a little bit more forthcoming when he addresses young men about marriage, cautioning them to make sure that they're healthy and that there's no trace left of that "old dose" before they walk down the aisle. Here's what he tells *them* about the wedding night: "Be tender, considerate, and appreciate that the little wife has had a day of excitement and nervous and physical strain. . . . She is absolutely yours and for the first time is entirely in your power. Do not shock her by indelicate treatment or you may make yourself forever repulsive to her." How to consummate the marriage still remains a secret. However, he does caution that newly married couples are "prone to overindulgence, little realizing the great injury they cause their nervous systems."

Since these pamphlets were sold as a set, it was just possible that children or unmarried women might be curious enough to read all of them. Sexual organs were eliminated because Hubbard had to be certain he never wrote or illustrated anything that might be inappropriate for "the little wife" or younger readers. For the same reason, anything that suggests impropriety, like, for example, the sex act itself, had to be either written around or ignored.

AN ICONOCLASTIC TRADITIONALIST

Hubbard fought against prohibition, believing the answer was education, not restriction. He testified in front of a Congressional committee on heroin, which was then commonly prescribed as a pain killer, because he understood it was too dangerously addictive to be legally available. He took on "quacks" who falsely promised miracle cures for everything from baldness and obesity to terminal disease, and taught how to identify and avoid them. And he was quixotic enough to consult on Cummins's films, even though it meant journalists and colleagues called him a "charlatan," because he recognized that the new medium of motion pictures was the best way to educate a widespread audience.

As a dermatologist, Hubbard saw numerous cases of gonorrhea and syphilis, not just in men but in the women and children who were collateral damage. In the days before antibiotics, these diseases had no cure and logically became what he wanted most to eradicate. Abortion was a close second. Both could have been almost completely prevented by the correct use of condoms, which had been available for more than sixty years. However, any method of birth control was prohibited by the 1873 Comstock Act, which wasn't revoked until 1936. Due to the firm belief by moralists of the time that access to contraception promoted promiscuity and lewd behavior, this law restricted sale of birth control products and even informational literature, either through the mail or across state lines. Two-thirds of the states restricted all sales of contraceptives. In Comstock's home state of Connecticut, it was even illegal for a married couple to use them. The anti-contraception faction was so strong that information about birth control was edited out of all post-1873 editions of medical textbooks. Many physicians, possibly even Hubbard, were ignorant on the subject. But ignorant or not, condom use was not something he could legally write about, even if he wanted to. (There is a terse reference to birth control in "Facts About Parenthood": "If at all possible it is wise to prevent conception during the nursing period of the new born. Regarding this your physician should advise you.") His opinion on abortion, however, was crystal clear: "The world holds no more cowardly murderers than those who are involved in committing abortions to prevent childbirth." Unless sex is specifically for procreation, or enjoyed with the airtight commitment that if pregnancy results you are a married couple prepared to love and nurture the baby, it should not be a part of your life. Abstinence is Hubbard's main line of defense and his one real "fact." In a world without antibiotics or legally available prophylactics, it was all he had.

THE SENSATIONAL MOTION PICTURE OF THE YEAR

Some Wild Oats was first released by Cummins in 1919. It was also called *Know Thy Husband*, which hints at the venereal disease aspects of the plot. It was one of at least eight new "sex hygiene" films released after the war. The stories were similar: A young man does something extremely foolish—he has illicit sex—and venereal disease destroys him and the innocent woman he loves.[3] Around this time, censorship began to be a strong factor in the film industry, making it a challenge to get distribution on films with controversial topics. Most early producers (such as the Warner brothers, who began their empire with this type of release) chose to abandon sensational material, which meant anything about sex, pregnancy, venereal disease, alcohol, or drugs. Those who remained produced lower-cost films that

---

3 Schaefer, p. 25.

were often of inferior quality. Moralistic in the extreme, they offered a peek into the secret world of the decadent and graphically showed why people foolish enough to go there were forever doomed. This was all very similar to a Hubbard pamphlet. Success depended upon walking a fine line between giving the public a tiny amount of titillation and still demonstrating sufficient educational value to remain open after the first screening. Since most censors believed that any mention of sexuality would cause moviegoers to behave lasciviously, they would shut down a film even if the wanton behavior resulted in devastation, deformity, and death (which, in a Cummins production, it always did). When *Some Wild Oats* opened at the Harris Theater on West Fifty-second Street in New York City, the theater's license was immediately revoked,[4] but it was soon allowed to reopen, mainly because of Dr. Hubbard's endorsement.

WATCH FOR OUR NEXT PRODUCTION!

Those words, on the back cover of every pamphlet, refer to *The Naked Truth*. The plot has a familiar ring to it: it's "the story of a fellow who sowed his Wild Oats." Quotes pulled from Hubbard's pamphlets were interspersed between action scenes and printed on the screen for all to read and hopefully memorize: "Fathers, tell your sons that some prostitutes are diseased all of the time, and nearly all prostitutes are diseased some of the time."[5] To give the film addi-

---

4 "Revokes Theater License." *New York Times*. June 5, 1920.

5 Schaefer, p. 171.

tional medical (and even fewer artistic) credentials, Cummins purchased footage from the American Social Hygiene Association, including diagrams of the human anatomy and horrific shots depicting the effects of syphilis and gonorrhea. The paralyzed, the blind, and the "idiots" were all featured, with subtitles like "parents had syphilis."[6] If there ever was a film that would stop *anyone* from wanting to sow wild oats, it was *The Naked Truth*. By 1927 it was playing in established theaters all over the country, with separate screenings for men and women. It was a blockbuster.[7]

When the Comstock laws were reversed in 1936, the surgeon general began a war on venereal disease. This was a perfect time for Cummins's work to enter the mainstream, and it did. His *Sex Madness* was paired on a popular double bill with Shirley Temple's *Wee Willie Winkie*."[8]

These pamphlets give us an opportunity to slow down, step back in time to nearly a century ago, and explore an amusing little piece of American history. But reading between the lines reveals Dr. Hubbard's apprehension about an America transitioning from a rural and traditional Victorian age to one more urban and less conventional. The centerpiece of this modern age was the successful new feminist movement and women's suffrage. When cigarette-smoking, short-

---

6 Ibid.

7 Schaefer, p. 170.

8 Briggs, Joe Bob. "Kroger Babb's Roadshow." November 2003. Accessed at: www.reason.com/news/show/28934.html.

skirted flappers tempted men with "petting parties" and flasks of illegal gin, they were early-twentieth-century sirens beckoning them into the future, opening up a forbidden world of sensuality and sexual equality for exploration.

It's easy to imagine why the idealistic Dr. Hubbard found all of this frightening. He knew the pitfalls, and he had two daughters. But he was ultimately a romantic too, writing: "Sex is intimately related to the best in art and sculpture" and "Love is the light, heat and power of the world."

Bob Berkowitz
Susan Yager-Berkowitz
New York, New York

SEX FACTS

FOR

YOUNG MEN

Prepared by

S. DANA HUBBARD, M.D.

NEW YORK

Attending Dermatologist to the
New York City Children's Hospital
Dermatologist Letchworth Village
Director
Bureau Public Health Education, New York City
Department of Health

SEX FACTS FOR YOUNG MEN ABOUT THE VENEREAL DISEASES.

Read What Professor Charles W. Eliot of Harvard says:—

"Chastity in a man is just as necessary as chastity in a woman for the country, for the honor and happiness of family life: continence is absolutely healthful for both sexes: men's profligacy is the cause or source of woman's prostitution, with its awful consequences to the guilty parties and to innocent human beings who are later infected by the guilty; the most precious joys and most durable satisfactions of life are put at a fearful risk by sexual immorality."

Public health is a question in which every citizen or coming citizen should be vitally interested at all times.

The more that is known about the matter of disease prevention, the better for all, as the more information the people get the more alert will all be to protect their own health and through this better the health of the community. No matter is more disastrous to public health than the venereal diseases. Its evil effects are far reaching. Ignorance is the greatest of all sins.

"Let There be Light."

Fore-word.

Tradition has handed much mis-information from generation to generation of boys and girls regarding their "Parts" and it is hoped that you through reading these words may be stimulated to seek light and knowledge about yourself, so that you may be physically and mentally fit.

In life's battle victory is with the strong—

body and mind—here and there cunning, wit, or chance may win a temporary victory but that which lasts is founded on perfect health.

Keeping fit and being in the best of condition at all times means that you must be healthy.

Are you in Condition?

Young man, why are you not always in condition?

When every child has healthy strong parents, and is born strong and well ,which is a birth right, then if these children are reared as the farmer rears his prize stock—these little ones will have a fair start in life. Not having it are they not seriously handicapped?

Some day you are going to be a man, you are going to marry and have children which is the natural order of human evolution. Are you looking ahead to see that your family will have a fine healthy father? If not your ears may be rubbing together.

How Vigorous Manhood is Achieved?

Those who would achieve the maximum vigor must observe at least five essentials.

1. Sufficient exercise of the right kind.

2. Sleep in fresh air, work in fresh air, live in fresh air.

3. Sleep at least eight hours, every night— seven nights in the week.

4. Eat proper food, regularly and chew your food well and eat slowly. Eat wisely.

5. To win vigorous manhood and retain it young men should be chaste.

Take it and be a regular fellow.

Exercise.

Exercise is absolutely essential to physical development. If you are out in the open watch the young colt, the young calf, or any living young thing and you will notice that it is on the go almost continually. It is hungry always and tires quickly and when play has been too strenuous, it eats and falls asleep immediately. Later it awakens and repeats this process day after day until fully grown.

The healthy child, boy or girl is full of vim, energy and go. If the child had as free run as the young animal and maternal instinct in the young mother was as keen as in the dog or cow or even the rabbit, we would see a different race in a few generations of human beings. Living artificially and away from nature these natural instincts are smothered and we do live an unnatural existence.

If the weather will not permit out door exercise, try general gymnasium work, boxing, wrestling or hand ball, but always see that the air is fresh.

A young man's daily exercise should be vigorous enough to cause perspiration (sweating) to come freely. This helps the body to throw off waste products which would act as poisons if allowed to accumulate within.

After exercise a bath should be taken. A shower is the best but if not available use a wash bowl, using warm water at first then cold water. The bath should be followed by a vigorous rub-down with a coarse towel. This bath and rub should not take over 5 minutes. It will make the body glow and give a general feeling of comfort and well being.

Fresh Air.

One of the essentials of life is air. We can do without food more or less indefinitely, we can go for days without water, but we cannot do without air for more than a few moments.

❧ Our bodies are peculiar chemical machines and can "get along" under almost impossible conditions but this abuse will tell with time. It is difficult to keep an account of health in the ledger of life and debit and credit the good and the bad but every abuse like sand in the oil scores the cylinder until compression is lost and power gone. The sand was a trifling thing it is true but it turned the trick.

Young men should sleep in the fresh air, not necessarily out of doors, although this is not dangerous. Night air is good air. No bed room is big enough to sleep in if the windows are closed. Work in the fresh air. Always see that your shop or office is well ventilated. Do not open windows and cause a draught but drop the upper sash a little or raise the lower an inch and put a board between the bottom sash and the jamb. While the crevice is small it will permit a large amount of fresh air to enter and circulate within as well as permitting the foul stale air, often times over heated, to escape. Be sure to keep the air within doors fresh during the day. Fresh air is nature's cure all. It is usually more valuable than the best of medicines.

Sleep.

Science has demonstrated that the amount of sleep required can be estimated most accurately. Young men need eight hours sleep every night and most boys between the ages of 13 and 16 years of age require eight and a half to nine and a half hours.

With less, one can get along, but he can not

keep himself in the best possible physical condition. One should not lie in bed after waking but jump out and dress immediately.

Proper Food.

Nothing is more essential to health and perfect physical development than proper diet, regularly taken and digested. One might also state truthfully that one of the very earliest signs of ill health is a capricious and delicate appetite.

Hunger is a positive sign of health—hunger is also present in disease but if a young man eats and enjoys his food we will not have to concern ourselves much about his health.

The appetite is the best judge of selection. If food tastes good and sits well then don't bother whether it will agree with one's stomach, but go to it and get your fill. Never Over Eat.

A young man should eat that which makes the body grow, and there is nothing better than fresh vegetables, cereals, especially oat meal, bread, preferably whole wheat bread, butter, eggs and ripe fruit, with meat or fish, not oftener than once a day. Drink a glass of milk daily.

The system needs not only the kind of food that is rich in nourishment, but food that provides bulk, like vegetables as this stimulates the action of the bowels. A horse and a cow will eat and eat straw and hay until one would think that they would drop in their tracks or that their jaws would ache like ours do when using chewing gum but this fodder is fine for the relief of sluggishness of the bowels.

You don't see our horses and cattle keeping drug shops busy selling cathartics. Not that they do not need cleaning out occasionally, but they are not so habitually constipated as are our young men. It would be splendid if science could find in the human dietry some thing as appealing to young people's appetite as does straw, hay and fodder to the appetitie of our humbler friends. It is true we have such food but our fastidious people who have strayed away from natural foods have acquired an artificial or aesthetic taste for white bread, and rich concentrated foods which cause sluggishness of the bowels and tend toward constipation. If we ate more rough food, whole wheat bread, corn bread, bran bread, rough oat meal, beans, and vegetables high in fibre, bowel atony would soon disappear. Water is an essential to any dietry. Every young man should drink habitually not less than 6 to 8 glasses of cool fresh wholesome water every day. Don't wash down your food with water but when your mouth is empty refresh yourself with a swallow or two. Drink slowly and never shock your stomach by taking cold water too quickly. Chilling the stomach retards digestion.

All food should be chewed to a pulp before swallowing.

Do not make it a habit to eat between meals.

Sweets are helpful in making heat within the body. In summer eat them sparingly and in winter use them only after meals and when fatigue (weariness) is acute. Remember how chocolate bars helped our dough-boys in the late war. Nevertheless do not over indulge in sweets.

Not only is it necessary to eat wisely but it is most important to pass off the waste materials by regular movements of the bowels. When this is not done, one becoming constipated, is likely to have headaches, sluggish muscular action and feel uncomfortable generally if not actually ill. Regular movements of the bowel are aided by an abundance of exercise and by eating plenty of fruit and drinking plenty of good water. When nature suggests action, always respond, as nothing begets irregularity of bowel action more than inattention to these sensations. Be regular and habituate yourself to a schedule and your bowels will respond. If we can "house-train" our pets why not similarly train ourselves? Nothing is more conductive to health and strength than regularity in bowel movement.

Chastity—The Relation of the Productive Organs to Vigor.

If a young man is to win vigorous manhood and retain it, it is important that he should understand fully the relationship of the reproductive organs to vigor. This needs to be carefully explained, because while the facts of themselves are important, they are not generally understood. Much misinformation is handed out about the facts of life to young people for this information is passed from ignorant pal to pal about his 'privates.'

It would not be possible for a small, immature boy to achieve the full vigor of manhood were it not for the stimulation generated by the glands of the reproductive or sex organs. This fact may be made clear by referring to the activity of the various glands in the body. Most of us are familiar with the action of the glands in the mouth, called the salvary glands and which secretes the fluid which not only helps lubricate our food while in the mouth but furnishes a ferment which aids in the partial digestion of certain of our foods (ptyalin in the saliva helps digest starches and sugars, this change being completed by the pancreatic juices further down in the intestines.)

In the upper and lower jaw on both sides of the face are sets of glands (maxillary parotid and lingual) which make secretions that aid us when we eat and help change the food so that it can be taken up by the blood.

These digestive glands are also in the abdomen accompanying the bowels and pour secretion into the intestinal canal and change the different components of the food so that it can be taken into the blood stream and furnished by the blood to the different parts requiring material for work.

There are other glands about which but little is known by science except in a very general way. These are the blind or ductless glands (called ductless because they have no duct to drain the secretion to other parts.) These blind glands—tonsils, thyroid, pineal, and others are located in different parts of the body,—the tonsils in the throat, the thyroid in the neck and the pineal in the head—at present the functions of these blind glands are enveloped in more or less mystery but there are various theories regarding their use.

When these glands are disturbed or are affected with disease we see certain definite changes in our body and hence we conclude that the functions are stimulating or restraining actions within the body.

The reproductive organs have two of these blind glands, in the males called testacles, and in the female called ovaries. These glands in addition to aiding in the process of reproduction also have a definite part in the development of the human body, not only in its physical growth but they also act on the brain in stimulating it to increased power of action and retention (memory). Also they stimulate the growth of this organ.

The condition of the mind has considerable to do with vigor. Various mental conditions often cause bodily changes. For instance; sorrow, a mental condition, may cause loss of appetite: Embarassment, a mental condition, may cause one to blush. Likewise ,if a boy or man permits himself to look at suggestive pictures or to listen to vulgar stories, or to indulge in lewd thoughts, he brings about a mental condition which is likely to result in evil practices, which may cause his ruin through acquiring venereal disease.

While it is not always possible to prevent these things coming to one's attention, it is possible, by self control, by using one's will power, to direct the attention away from these harmful influences and center thoughts on wholesome subjects.

Some young men will need to learn the trick of switching the thoughts away from suggestive subjects quickly to sports, school work, or other helpful activities. The mind should not be made a cess pool but a reservoir of thoughts helpful to self and others.

The Many Menaces to Manly Vigor.

It seems timely to refer in some detail to two diseases which are caused by mis-use of the reproductive organs because many men do not understand how serious these really are and how easily they are acquired.

These diseases are called Gonorrhoea and Syphilis. In popular terminology they are known as "clap" and "pox". They are caused by sexual intercourse with lewd women—women and girls who sell themselves to men to gratify lust.

The experience in New York, where a large number of these clandestine and public prostitutes (whores) have been carefully examined by physicians employed by the city, has shown that eighty per cent of these women are diseased all of the time and all of them some of the time.

Gonorrhoea is often apparently cured in a few weeks' time, but the germs may remain in the body more or less indefinitely. Years afterward serious complications may manifest themselves in the man, or the man thinking himself cured may give the disease to his wife, who through such infection may be crippled for life or may become sterile (Gonorrhoea causing pus sacs and closing the tubes, or who, when baby is born may communicate the germs to the eyes of the infant and cause it to go blind either at birth or shortly after birth. Over one-fourth of the cases of blindness in this country have been traced directly to gonorrhoea.

Syphilis is in some respects even worse, for it may cause personal disfiguration, (destruction of the bones) or it may cause insanity or paralysis in the man, or terrible afflictions to his children. A very large percentage of our feeble minded children are offspring of syphilitic fathers.

Though some ignorant or uninformed men hold that sexual intercourse is necessary to physical health, this is contrary to the best medical authority in this country and abroad. The leading medical specialists in diseases of men declare that there is no evidence to sustain the statement that sexual indulgence is necessary or that abstinence from sex activity is "inconsistent with the highest physical, mental and moral efficiency."

Men who act upon this false idea of sex often find out to their sorrow that sexual intercourse has resulted in disease and not health.

When a wrestler, boxer or prize fighter is training for a contest and needs all the vigor and endurance possible, trainers invariable insist upon abstinence from sexual activity.

While it is important for a young man to understand all of these facts, it is not necessary for him to remember all the details to which we have referred in our endeavors to impress our conclusions. In fact it would be best to dismiss these matters from mental consideration. The important thing to do is to lead a vigorous active life, taking excellent care of himself, and leave nature to do the rest.

What Fitness Demands.

Physical fitness demands:—
1. Muscular strength.
2. Endurance.
3. Energy.
4. Will Power.
5. Courage.
6. Self Control.

To be in prime physical condition and to keep fit is the highest ambition of every normal young man and boy. By intensive athletic training a man may become a sprinter or a successful foot ball player or succeed in any other special sport. The wiser aim for most men and boys would be to be always in condition for any kind of sport, any

NAMES OF MALE PARTS.

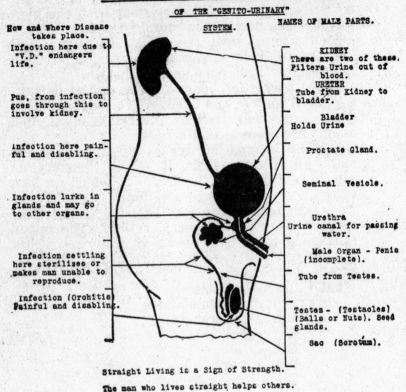

How and Where Disease takes place.

Infection here due to "V.D." endangers life.

Pus, from infection goes through this to involve kidney.

Infection here painful and disabling.

Infection lurks in glands and may go to other organs.

Infection settling here sterilizes or makes man unable to reproduce.

Infection (Orchitis) Painful and disabling.

KIDNEY
There are two of these. Filters Urine out of blood.

URETER
Tube from Kidney to bladder.

Bladder
Holds Urine

Prostate Gland.

Seminal Vesicle.

Urethra
Urine canal for passing water.

Male Organ - Penis (incomplete).

Tube from Testes.

Testes - (Testacles) (Balls or Nuts). Seed glands.

Sac (Scrotum).

Straight Living is a Sign of Strength.

The man who lives straight helps others.

DR. HUBBARD'S SEX FACTS

kind of work, and any task a man may be called upon to perform.

,The reward of keeping fit is vigorous manhood and all the pleasure and comfort that comes from being healthy.

The Male Generative Organism.

The male generative organs are diagrammatically illustrated and the arrangement of the parts graphically demonstrated as if the body was bisected vertically, showing a cross section from front to rear.

The system is technically known as the Genito-Urinary organs because the excretory system and the reproductive system are inter-twined and work in some of the parts together.

Along the back, on each side of the bony spine about the level of the hips there are two bean shaped organs, the kidneys. Their function is to eliminate waste products from the blood stream and pass it off by way of the bladder and the male organ, the penis.

Disease of the kidneys is technically known as Nephritis (popularly termed Bright's Disease). Passing from the center of the kidneys are small tubes leading to base of bladder, these are the ureters and are often the seat of stone formation. In the front of the bony pelvis, at lower part of abdomen is located a thick muscular organ which is a reservoir for the urine, called the bladder. This has a capacity of about 10 to 15 ounces, though in diseased conditions the bladder has been known to hold a quart or more. Disease of the bladder is known as Cystitis.

At the base of the bladder and about the opening is a large "blind" gland called the prostate—

this in elderly persons becomes distended and interferes with the free passage of the urine.

The tube leading from the bladder to the outer world is the urethra, and is one of the compotent parts of the male organ, the penis. (In slang language called a "tool").

In the crotch of the thighs and in front of the anal opening is a loose muscular sac, called the scrotum (in slang parlance it is called the 'bag') In this sac are the male organs of reproduction, the testes (popularly called 'nuts'). The sac is divided by a membrane making it into two parts, one part hanging a little below the other, this is a natural arrangement because in this way it prevents injury to the sensitive testes and aids them in sliding out of the way of harm when any pressure is exerted likely to compress or squeeze them.

The testes secrete the seminal or life fluid of the male.

The testes are connected to the base of the bladder by cords known as the spermatic cords. In this cord are arteries, nerves and veins as well as absorbents known as lymphatics.

In preventing conception by males an operation known as Vasectomy is performed which cuts or obstructs this cord and thereby sterilizes the male, making it impossible for him to reproduce. It is an essential one in the case of epileptics, chronic tubercular (consumptives) invalids, and in the feeble-minded and idiotic.

There are two glands in the urethra, called Cowper's, about the size of a pea, one is situated on each side of the canal and secrete a mucous albuminous fluid, the function of which is to lubricate and cleanse the canal and render innocuous any material injurious to the spermatozoa.

At the bottom of the bladder on each side of the opening and about opposite to the prostate gland are two small pouches the seminal vesicles which serve as reservoirs for the semen and also secrete a fluid which dilutes this material. The opening of these into the urethra has two ducts, one on each side, and these have great muscular power causing the throwing out of this material. These are known as the ejaculatory ducts.

The male seminal fluid is known as semen, secreted by the testes, stored in the reservoirs, the seminal vesicles and consists of a rather transparent, colorless glycerine-like fluid, slightly albuminous (white of egg) like odor and in this is the life germ the spermatozoa. These are living elements and very minute in size.

The intromittent organ or organ used in conducting the urine from the body to the outer world is the Penis and consists of erectile tissue arranged in three cylindrical compartments—like a two barrelled shot gun with its ramrod—urethra—underneath. It terminates in a bulbuous body known as the "Glans Penis" which is covered by a prolongation of the soft skin known as the 'fore-skin' or prepuce.

Gonorrhoea infection attacks the lining of the urethra and causes an intense inflammation accompanied by a thick yellowish discharge, which as the disease becomes chronic, turns to a pale whitish color, it is then known as "Gleet".

If the inflammation of the urethra incident to the gonorrhoea excites ulceration it may bend the organ causing Cordae.

If this ulcer corrodes or destroys the tissue of the canal this bending may be permanent when sexual relations will be either difficult, painful or impossible.

This ulceration of the urethra on healing leaves a scar, which through contracting, as all scars do, lessens the calibre of the canal causing "stricture" which may be partial or complete. When complete it prevents passage of the urine and a painful and serious operation must be performed to open the canal.

REPRODUCTION.

Most young men are ignorant of the true facts in the hygiene of the reproductive organs and of the diseases with which they may become infected.

What knowledge they may have gained has usually been obtained from equally ignorant companions, through their own secret experiences, or through the medium of pamphlets issued by advertising "quacks" or so-called 'Men's Specialists,' who claim that they can cure sex diseases.

This information is often times so exaggerated and so misleading that it is safe to assert that it is entirely false and mercenary, as it is the desire of the advertiser to sell either his advice or his ware.

The first function of the sex or reproductive organs is to develop the boy intc a vigorous man. The other function is to enable him to reproduce his kind when he becomes mature and the head of a family..

By the process of reproduction, all forms of life, flowers, trees, birds, fish, wild and domestic animals, and human beings—are perpetuated on the earth. If the function of reproduction did not exist in life, the earth would soon become barren. Reproduction therefore is essential and it is important to understand how life is passed from one generation to another.

PLANT LIFE.

In many forms of plant life the flower contains the reproductive organs. The flower changes into the seed and so they are kept through the cold season and when planted in the spring they reproduce like the one from which they came.

ANIMAL LIFE.

A most interesting example of animal reproduction is furnished in the deep sea fish, the salmon. In the spring they swim into rivers, jumping at times up high water falls and enter shallow sheltered places for nests. There the female lays a quantity of eggs. The male comes to the nest and deposits from his body a quantity of fertilizing fluid containing cells called sperms. Many of the eggs fertilized develop into fish.

The male and the female salmon are however exhausted by the process of reproduction, drift down stream in a more or less helpless condition and many never reach the ocean alive, giving up their lives, as it were, to reproduce their young.

HUMAN LIFE.

Human reproduction is similar in many ways to the reproduction in the flower. Inside the human mother's body are minute germ cells called ova. ·In the male organs there are other minute germ cells called sperms. When a sperm comes in contact with an ovum inside of the mother's body it fertilizes it, thus making it capable of growing. It develops, protected by the mother's body, and nourished by the blood from her heart, it slowly takes human form and after nine months of growth, it has sufficient strength to live and is then born into the world.

In plant life reproduction is largely dependent upon the action of bees, the wind, and other natural forces. In animal life reproduction is almost automatic. The salmon simply obeys the reproductive instinct when spring time comes. Man has the reproductive instinct, but he has acquired the power to control this faculty. The sex instinct may be a source of destruction or a great blessing. If it is abused, disease and suffering may result. If it is understood and controlled it becomes a source of added strength and a richer and fuller life.

The sex instinct may be compared to other natural forces in life. Fire is a great blessing to mankind. It warms our houses, and through its force machinery moves the world. When fire is controlled it is a valuable aid but let it get beyond control and it wrecks and causes ruin and destruction. So sex energy must be controlled and directed. The youth entering manhood needs the full power of his will to keep his sex desires from leading him astray and leading him into habits that will not only weaken him physically and mentally but may through venereal disease cause his destruction and that of his wife if he has one, or some woman who has given him her trust.

The Young Man's Relationship to Girls.

The young man should think of all girls as the future mothers of the race and understand that one of their most important functions in life is to become the mother of healthy children who will make helpful and useful citizens of tomorrow.

A nation is judged by its attitude toward its women.

The youth who is fair, who is honorable, who is a sportsman, will treat every girl as he expects others to treat his own sister.

Every man who has any principle believes in fair play. He despises cheating. The young man who is fair will adopt for his own life the same standard he demands of the woman he expects to marry some day. Each youth who grows up and marries becomes a link in a great social chain of human beings. This chain connects the years of yesterday with the decades of tomorrow. One false step may infect the racial stock and blight the lives of generations to come. The spark of life is to be accepted as a sacred trust to be transmitted undimmed to future generations.

Sex Hygiene.

Self-Abuse, Masturbation.

A great many young men have at some time been victims of the habit of artificially stimulating their sexual organs. If this habit is continued it leads to physical and mental weakness, but if it is stopped, as it usually is, before it is done to excess, it need give no further anxiety.

To have vigor and mental health this habit must be discontinued. If continuously indulged in, it will result in permanent injury to health and mental capacity.

"Wet Dreams", Seminal Emissions.

Nightly emissions, or "wet dreams" occur in perfectly healthy young men: they do not indicate an unhealthy condition of the sexual organs.

It is simply nature's method of emptying an over-filled gland.

The "Quacks" take advantage of the known ignorance of boys and young men of this fact, and make use of it to frighten them into paying large sums of money for unnecessary treatment.

A young man who exercises vigorously, eats moderately, and refrains from alcohoic drinking and who does not allow himself to yield to sexual excitement, in thought or deed, NEED NEVER WORRY ABOUT NOCTURNAL SEMINAL EMISSIONS.

A frequently repeated statement made by the quack and imposter is that these nightly emissions are indicative of loss of manhood but such is a gross and wilful lie and made knowingly to deceive the uninformed.

Swollen or Distended Veins—Varicocele.

The bag or sac located behind the male organ of reproduction contains arteries, veins, and the blind glands known as the testacles (called 'balls' or 'nuts' by the man-of-the-street). The veins sometimes weaken and become very much distended, forming a mass or tumor. This is called technically a varicocele and means that the veins of the testacle have become distended like those in the lower limbs often do when excessive stimulation is indulged in.

There are many causes for varicocele but none of serious moment. Pressure by bandaging may relieve the condition or the veins may be tied by a surgeon in a simple though delicate operation. A cure is aways possible.

Undescended Testacle.

At times and apparently without any special

reason one of the blind glands—testacle—may not enter the sac as puberty approaches—tenth to fourteenth year of age—but may be retained in the canal in the abdominal wall. This is not serious. An operation may be necessary to place the gland in its right place or it may be left as nature deposited it. It is a matter of whether the failure to descend causes any particular discomfort or not. Leave it alone unless physical discomfort is experienced.

Some have concluded that this failure to descend may later lead to an enlargement of the canal and produce a rupture (hernia). Some times this does occur but many times it does not.

Venereal Disease. Gonorrhoea, Syphilis.

Sexual indulgence outside of the marriage relation often leads to infection with one or more of the venereal diseases.

All women who are loose or have 'easy virtue' pubic or private, sooner or later acquire one or both of the venereal diseases.

The man who exposes himself to these women is in constant danger of ruining his health.

The "Private snap" or occasional prostitute or clandestine woman of easy morals is often the most dangerous of the species.

It must be appreciated that a woman who submits to these embraces with one man either on short acquaintance or for a consideration—money or presents—will 'fall' for another. This promiscuousness leads to infection and transmission of disease.

Syphilis. Big "Pox," Lues, Rale, "Blood Disease," Etc.

In America this is called the French disease and

In continental Europe it is called the Western Disease. But call it what one may it is best to agree upon a term and arbitrarily adhere to it.

Throughout the world it is known as syphilis. We shall call it by its well known title.

Syphilis is an infectious disease of the blood: this infection spreads to all parts of the body. It is nearly always acquired through illicit sexual intercourse. Occásionally it may be acquired through kissing or from the use of a common drinking cup or common towel.

There are numerous instances recorded where using another's pipe, knife, fork, spoon, or eating out of a dish with others has passed syphilis from the sick to the well.

At first syphilis appears as a small sore, at the point of entrance (inoculation) and at this time may seem to be of no serious consequence. The first lesion—the sore—is called "A Hard Chancre." This usually occurs when there is a lesion or opening affording entrance to the germs.

Syphilis is one of the most dangerous diseases with which one can become infected. Its more serious effects may often not be apparent until many years—often twenty or more—after infection, and it affects not only the individual himself but also his children and grand-children, "even unto the third and fourth generation."

Syphilis is the cause of locomotor ataxia and is one of the most frequent causes of insanity (Paresis) and other diseases of the brain.

Syphilis very often causes diseases of the heart and blood vessels, resulting in sudden death.

Syphilis not only greatly decreases one's earning capacity, but it decreases the length of life about one-third.

The Wasserman re-action of the blood is now counted upon to determine the presence of syphilis and to aid in determining when it is cured.

The introduction of a preparation of arsenic known popularly as "606"—Salvarsan—has overcome the germs in a way but not wholly so.

Virtue is its own reward, because moral living promotes health while conversely, impure living often results in disease.

Is it a square deal for a man to demand purity in his wife when he may be harboring germs of syphilis that may blind or blight their off-spring?

Self command and strong will are elements of character independent of sex. The weak minded are notably weak in regard to sex matters, and in this direction have little or no judgment and offer no resistence to temptation.

There is no reason to limit the term prostitute to the female. Why not call a spade, a spade? Roue, rake, roter and debauche may be more masculine but they convey the same idea of loose morals.

Moral laxity has often been explained if not advocated upon physiological grounds, but this is merely the excuse of those who do not wish to keep within the bounds of the pale of purity.

Sex necessity is a myth.

The same passion that has, uncontrolled, made libertines of some individuals, has by conjugal love and good-will been softened and transformed to the perfecting of thousands of other men.

The life of both man and woman is a process of evolution, only developing properly under the en-

nobling influence of a permanent union, to which
the advent of children adds responsibilities, and
cements the affections and purifies the sex relations.

Gonorrhoea, "Clap", "A Dose".

The other sex disease (venereal disease) against
which young men and boys need be warned is
Gonorrhoea.

These venereal diseases, if comparisons are possible ,may be said to be the very worst of all of the
infections.

They are germ diseases, which are readily communicable—"catching"—and are caught from
other persons who have them,—usually from pros-
titues—or girls who only occasionally have sex
relations with men and boys. Such women and
girls are to be pitied and to be avoided. They
are an open menace to health.

Gonorrhoea (clap) is usually a local disease of
the urinary passage, but it is far from "being
no worse than a cold," as is commonly supposed.

Gonorrhoea may become a blood disease and
cause a very severe kind of 'rheumatism' and
sometimes even death.

Gonorrhoea often leads to stricture or closing
off of the urinary canal so that the urine can not
flow: this stoppage can only be relieved by a painful and disabling operation.

Gonorrhoea, like syphilis, may be transmitted
later to a man's wife, even long after he thinks
he is cured.

Gonorrhoea in a woman or girl is a still more serious disease than it is in a man. It is the cause
of hundreds of thousands of operations on the
female generative organs. It often causes blind-

ness in new born babies, and much of all the blindness in the world. It has been said that one-fourth of the blindness in this country is due to gonorrhoea.

Gonorrhoea often leads to sterility in both men and women.

Gonorrhoea is the chief cause of childless marriages.

If you are so unfortunate as to have this disease, consult a reliable physician or your local health officer and continue under treatment until advised that no further treatment is necessary. Never stop and take chances until a reliable physician advises that you are cured.

Facts to Remember about Gonorrhoea.

Gonorrhoea is one of the most prevalent of the communicable diseases—it is said to be even more prevalent than measles the most common and frequent disease of childhood.

Gonorrhoea affects both sexes, all ages and all classes of society. The rich and the poor, the educated and the ignorant. It does not respect caste, wealth or station.

Gonorrhoea has been estimated to have caused one-fourth of all the cases of total blindness in this country.

Gonorrhoea is the cause of four-fifths of the blindness of the new-born.

Gonorrhoea is the cause of numberless thousands of operations on the female generative organs.

Gonorrhoea is the cause of more than half of the cases of sterility—childless marriages.

Gonorrhoea is the cause of many chronic diseases of the joints, bladder and generative organs.

Gonorrhoea causes idleness and decreases one's earning capacity considerably.

Gonorrhoea is the underlying cause of untold misery for much of the unhappiness of married life is due to gonorrhoea.

Gonorrhoea affects practically all prostitutes, public and clandestine.

Gonorrhoea may be cured but it requires careful medical skill.

Gonorrhoea is a communicable disease and is readily preventable if the known rules of sanitary science are heeded.

Facts to Remember About Syphilis. The Pox.

Syphilis in one of its varied forms affects between 8 and 10% of our people, perhaps more.

Syphilis respects neither sex, race, nor social relations.

Syphilis is the cause of one-fourth of the cases of insanity.

Syphilis is one of the principal causes of mentally defective children, idiocy and imbecility.

Syphilis causes Locomotor Ataxia—serious and progressive form of paralysis of the arms and legs.

Syphilis causes softening of the brain in numberless thousands of instances in men and women. Paresis.

Syphilis is one of the chief causes of a "Stroke" in early life followed by a temporary paralysis.

Syphilis is the cause of nearly one half of the abortions and of nearly four-fifths of the still births.

Syphilis is the cause of many diseases of the heart and blood vessels and of many of the other vital organs.

Syphilis shortens life about one-third.

Syphilis greatly decreases one's earning capacity—the loss of time in industry due to syphilis is only equalled by accidents.

Syphilis is the underlying cause of pain, misery, suffering, mental anguish, and unhappiness.

Syphilis affects many prostitutes, public and clandestine.

Syphilis is a readily communicable disease.

Syphilis is a preventable disease.

Definition of Terms.

Self-abuse is a common expression for the term Masturbation, which is used to designate the excitement of the sex organs by friction, usually with the hand ,in the male, and with the finger, or a candle in the case of the female.

Seminal-emissions is the phrase for an involuntary discharge of seminal fluid from the sex organs of the male.

Lost Manhood—is a slang phrase to denote inability to sustain an erection to effect entrance or to withhold ejaculation before or shortly after effecting entrance.

Gonorrhoea is vulgarly called "A dose", "The Clap," it produces an inflammation of the lining membranes of the male and female sex organs and may extend into the deeper tissues.

Gleet is a slang phrase for a chronic stage of gonorrhoea.

Venereal Disease is a term usually used to denote Gonorrhoea or Syphilis.

Syphilis is also called pox, lues, "blood Poison", and many other names. It is a dangerous communicable disease due to a germ—a spirillum, called the spirochetae Pallida because it is a crystalline white spiral, requiring a special apparatus —dark field and high illumination and a high powered microscope to view it.

Urethral Stricture means an abnormal narrowing of the canal which conveys urine from the bladder to the outer world.

Infection is a medical term generally used to designate the process by which living disease-producing germs, after gaining entrance to the body, grow and injure the tissues.

Apoplexy refers to sudden paralysis and profound stupor due to bleeding into the brain or spinal cord.

Paralysis means a loss of motion or sensation in some part of the body.

Insanity means a disorder of the mental faculties more or less permanent in character but without loss of consciousness or will.

Locomotor Ataxia means failure of the muscular coordination and other changes due to degeneration of certain parts of the spinal card and sensory nerves.

Self-Disinfection in the Prevention of Venereal Diseases.

The statistics on which this method has been advocated, "from the largest London Clinic" estimate that about 25% (one-fourth) of the cases of venereal disease had used immediate self-disinfection, which would indicate that but little if any reliance could be placed on this measure as a protection against contracting these diseases.

At the London Hospital authoritative figures give the percentage as 18. which may be considered an underestimate if any thing, and the first figures quoted may be a trifle high, but the two statements from such sources furnish information that may be accepted as a general guide.

When it is appreciated that venereal disease often occurs in boys and girls of 14 to 18 years of age, it is impractical to teach disinfection at these ages and therefore to be a valuable adjunct in control of these diseases this method is of negative value.

The carrying of disinfectants on the person, is a continual incitement to illicit intercourse and this is an argument against recommending this procedure, but of course it is entirely a question of personal opinion, as many hold varying views, some for and many against. Sufficient it is to state that self-disinfection is satisfactory in the majority of instances but in women it is a decided failure, failure no doubt being incident to imperfect instruction or inability to carry the procedure recommended into effect.

Men often consider these disinfectants recommended to prevent as sure cure remedies, whereas they are not and this complication leads to much misinformation and neglect to properly treat these infections.

Self-disinfection carried out with disinfectants of suitable strength and according to suitable instruction is valuable in preventing infection, but these conditions rarely if ever are found and so render this so-called 'safety' a danger to those who would expose themselves while holding to these views.

SEX FACTS

FOR THE

ADOLESCENT and MATURED WOMAN

Prepared by

S. DANA HUBBARD, M.D.
New York

Attending Dermatologist to the
New York City Children's Hospital
Dermatologist Letchworth Village
Director
Bureau Public Health Education, New York City
Department of Health

SEX FACTS FOR THE ADOLESCENT AND MATURED WOMAN.

Introductory.

We ask the careful reading, discussion and consideration of this essay—which is a compilation of the facts used by Federal, State and Municipal Public Health Officials, in an effort to PREVENT THE VENEREAL DISEASES—by Mothers and Fathers, by Educators, by Physicians, and all others whose hearts and heads are inclined towards our sincere and earnest efforts in the welfare of the BOY AND GIRL of today and the future generations of AMERICAN CHILDREN.

———o———

Woman's crowning jewel, the star of the setting, is modesty. Modesty infers innocence not ignorance.

———o———

Sex Differences.

Sex is a word of wonderful meaning. To a sallow, sorrowful spinster it suggests sin, and savors of the sewer; to a ruddy roister it implies a riot of debauchery and self-indulgence in sensuous pleasure: to the normal person—sound in mind and clean in body—sex signifies the profound and marvelous fact that running through nature there are two sorts of beings, the male and the female, and without their union neither of the former would be perpetuated.

The distinctions of sex are to be found in the anatomy and psysiology of all the animal kingdom, the head of which is mankind. Sex influences the aims, actions, deportment, mentality, behavior and character. Sex contains all. If any thing is sacred, the human body is sacred, and the glory and sweat of man is the token of manhood untainted and in woman a body clean, firm-fibred and beautiful in face and form.

Woman contains all qualities and tempers them, in her place all moves with balance. She is all things duly veil'd. The chastity of paternity therefore should match the sublime chastity of maternity.

Men and women naturally have many points in common, both physical and mental yet there is a vast difference between the two sexes.

I—What are Venereal Diseases?

They are dangerous germ diseases of the genital or sex organs of men and women the effects of which spread to other parts of the body and to future generations.

They are very old and very common diseases.

They are "catching" or communicable from the sick to the well. They are usually given by infected men and women in sexual relation outside of marriage.

The two principal venereal diseases are syphilis and gonorrhoea. Syphilis is styled by the uninformed as 'Pox', while Gonorrhoea is called 'clap.' There are other vulgar or slang names for them.

II—What are the Signs or Symptoms of Syphilis?

They are variable and have no regular sequence. Syphilis may imitate and be mistaken for any of the well-known diseases of the skin and internal organs and is with great difficulty at times properly identified.

Syphilis usually begins as a small sore on or near the sex organs, or it may appear on the lips or inside of the mouth. It always occurs at the site of entry of the germ into the body.

A rash on the skin or an ulcer may develop from the initial sore, or it may disappear after a few weeks but the disease, unless treated, is spread through the blood and becomes deep seated in the body.

Some times this initial sore or ulcer causes the skin or flesh to decay.

Ordinary pimples, black heads (Acne) and skin rashes do not indicate syphilis and their presence should not cause undue alarm.

III—What are the Signs and Symptoms of Gonorrhoea?

Gonorrhoea usually causes inflammation or soreness of the female sex organs, followed by burning pains and a thick yellowish discharge after the infection has started.

Discharge which women and girls know as "The Whites" (technically termed Leucorrhoea) does not always mean gonorrhoea. It is difficult without microscopical examination to differentiate between the two diseases. Some times a pale discharge indicates "the whites", a minor disease, frequently affecting women and girls who are in a run down condition or are over worked. Leucorrhoea ("the whites") is by no means so dangerous as gonorrheoa, but a girl suffering from such a discharge should seek proper treatment as some times this discharge hides the dangerous gonorrhoea germs.

Consult your physician, preferably a well informed woman doctor or seek confidential advice of your local health nurse.

IV—What are the effects of these Venereal Diseases.

Syphilis causes: Certain forms of insanity, including softening of the brain or paresis: loco-motor ataxia and some other forms of paralysis: weak minded and defective children: many deaths in infancy and many still-births.

Gonorrhoea causes: Blindness among babies born of diseased parents: many operations on women, and inability to bear children (sterility): certain forms of rheumatism: Certain forms of disease of the joints, bladder, and vital organs of reproduction: Gonorrhoea causes much life long sickness in both men and women: suffering, mis-ery, and unhappy lives generally.

Syphilis and Gonorrheoa, being germ diseases, must be properly treated to be cured. They do not leave the human body unaided: they do not disappear of their own accord.

V—How do Girls and Women Get These Diseases?

Usually—and in the great majority of instances —these diseases are contracted through wrongful (illicit) sex intercourse, or by marrying a man who has had one or both of these diseases and has not been cured.

Some times they are contracted from articles used in common with other persons, such as:— Drinking cups, towels, brushes, eating utensils, or at toilets used by a diseased person. Occasionally a girl may contract syphilis by kissing. The germs live best in the moist membrane lining the sex organs, the mouth, the throat, and the eyes.

Often syphilitic mothers give birth to syphilitic babies.

Frequently babies' eyes become infected with gonorrhoea germs while being born, and blindness may result. One quarter of the blindness of this country has been attributed to the infection of gonorrhoea.

VI—How can a Person Avoid the Venereal Disease?

By being careful about using public toilets, and never using personal articles about your face or your body that are not your own. Never use another's towel, tooth brush ,knife, fork or spoon, and never drink after another out of a common drinking cup or glass.

By avoiding sex relation outside of marriage. Men who take unreasonable liberties with girls usually have exposed themselves to these diseases through promiscuous association with prostitutes.

Almost all women who make a practice of improperly consorting sexually with men are infected with one or both of these diseases. No girl or woman can afford to take a chance with a man who proposes sex relations outside of marriage. When marrying, a woman should make sure that the man whom she is going to marry is not infected. The public law in many states demand these facts. Equally important it is that the woman be not infected. Many states now require a medical certificate to this effect from both contracting parties to a marriage when issuing a license to marry. The reason for this is that venereal diseases, so dangerous to future generations, may be prevented and those existing may be cured. There are many men and women free from these diseases, but there are also many who are infected.

The Young Girl's Part.

In the first place, if you have the idea in your head, that there is any thing 'horrid' or 'nasty' about sex matters get rid of that idea forever.

Nature sees to it that the world is full of people. Plants have sex as well as animals. Sex is a scheme for making and bringing together two tiny scraps, we call germ cells, from which every new life starts. Sex is a natural law just as growing up is.

It is true in large part that when you go out into the world you can never be sure of any body, but all men are not bad nor all women. In fact if the truth be known, it is very small and minor number who are antisocial in their morality. There are lots of fine men who are moral and live clean lives and the best part of it is that every year their numbers increase. It is unfair to condemn, as it is silly to trust, all men.

A girl cannot afford to be ignorant of sex matters, the world is getting to understand these problems more and more clearly as we have to face the unpleasant facts as the result of the spreading of the venereal diseases. In making effort in this direction we are building a finer, cleaner, ideal of sex and are gradually learning that the only safe and true way of treating the creative force in this world, is to see to it that all people have an opportunity for healthy bodies, for the right kind of fun, and a better understanding of themselves.

Why Young Girls Should Know Sex Facts?

The 'Lounge Lizard' who seeks to ruin a girl uses all the cunning that human ingenuity can devise, and appreciating woman's affectability he plays upon this emotion, ingratiating himself by making gifts and escorting the girl to those places where he knows she likes to go and have a good time.

An educated and informed girl however is a match for these despoilers and playing the game knows when to use trumps. Girls must be taught that it is not wrong to know sex facts, the wrong consists in making improper use of this information. 'If I had only known,' is an oft repeated remark of the unfortunate female who has been caught and despoiled. It is true if she had known she would not have permitted these personal liberties to have so pitilessly embarassed her.

The great mistake in sex education is when we go to the wrong source for information, or when we let the thing worry or bother us until we become restless or morbid; or worse, when we listen to risque or unclean stories and keep up a sort of vulgar and cheap excitement over sex matters. There is nothing which destroys one's good taste and imagination more quickly than a 'smutty' vulgar attitude towards sex. A girl must be on her guard against acquaintances who deal in this sort of stuff. Mental qualities may be quite as catching as diseases and are even less easily cured. **Facts For Young Women.**

An artificial way of looking at natural things has created a false modesty among many people and such delicate subjects as the hygiene and diseases of sex are often not spoken of by women, even in the privacy of the home. As a result, most mothers, instead of giving their daughters proper instruction in these matters, so that they can protect themselves, have too often thrown an atmosphere of mystery around these questions, with the hope that Providence, or some other unknown protective influence, would guard them **from harm.**

The vast majority of girls have thus grown to adolesence or even young womanhood entirely lacking in intelligent information on every thing relating to sex and maternity. Because of this ignorance many innocent maidens have been escorted to the alter of marriage by men already diseased (but equally as ignorant as themselves) and their subsequent health and happiness have been destroyed. In the place of a blissful and happy married life with a home endeared by healthy children, they have been condemned to a miserable existence, to sickness, suffering, sterility, and often an untimely death.

Is it not time, with our knowledge of these facts, that some thing should be done to change this deplorable condition? Is it not time that women should look the sex problem squarely in the face, devoid of mystery and so-called 'moral' issues, from a practical and common sense point of view? Is it not time that all girls and young women, the future mothers of our race, should know the truth about the reproducuive organs and diseases which may affect them, so as to preserve their health and that of their off-spring? It is the object of these essays to teach young women some f the facts which they should know about these ital things.

he Female Organs of Generation.

Every young woman should have at least an elementary knowledge of the anatomy and phyology of the reproductive organs in order that he may understand the importance of properly caring for them and protecting them from all harm.

The principal internal organ of generation of

This Outline Shows The Female Internal Organs
Of Reproduction. Demonstrating Crudely The
Parts Concerned with Menstruation.

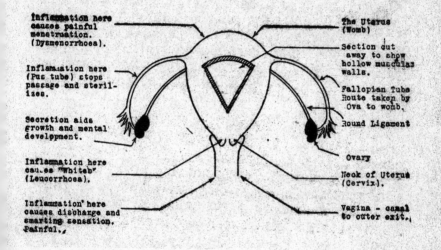

Inflammation here
causes painful
menstruation.
(Dysmenorrhoea).

Inflammation here
(Pus tube) stops
passage and steril-
izes.

Secretion aids
growth and mental
development.

Inflammation here
causes "Whites"
(Leucorrhoea).

Inflammation here
causes discharge and
smarting sensation.
Painful.,

The Uterus
(Womb)

Section cut
away to show
hollow muscular
walls.

Fallopian Tube
Route taken by
Ova to womb.

Round Ligament

Ovary

Neck of Uterus
(Cervix).

Vagina - canal
to outer exit.

WOMEN

the woman is the 'Womb' or as it is technically called the Uterus. This is located in the middle of the bony pelvic cavity at the lower part of the trunk. There are two ovaries—blind, ductless glands—located one on either side of the womb. The womb looks something like a Sickle pear with the point looking downward and is slightly flattened from front to back. It is a hard muscular organ. The ovaries which are about the size of almonds are filled with tiny eggs, called 'ova.' The ovaries are connected by means of fine tubes with the womb, one on the right and one on the left, and these are called the Fallopian Tubes. The ovaries secrete the ovum or egg which when discharged passes through the Fallopian tube into the womb. Here it stops, if fertilized by the male cell,—the sperm—and becomes the embryo or rudiamentary living child. If not previously fertilized, the ovum escapes and passes out with the menstrual flow.

At regular intervals the uterus is given an extra supply of blood so that in this way, if the ovum is fertile, it receives the necessary nourishment for the development of the embryo. If the ovum is not fertile, the uterus has no need for this extra amount of blood and it is expelled with the menstrual flow.

When a girl reaches her thirteenth or fourteenth year of age the process of menstruation usually begins, taking place every four weeks, and continuing regularly except during pregnancy, until the woman is about 45 years of age. At this time the menstrual flow finds the womb in a highly sensitive condition and it is easily disturbed by such influences as violent exercise, exposure to cold, or wet, etc.

On the first day of the monthly period, therefore girls should keep perfectly quiet, and they should abstain from exercise or exposure. Not heeding this there is likely to be a disarrangement of this function with either too little flow or too great and the period is then accompanied by considerable pain and discomfort, especially back ache. This is technically termed Dysmenorrhoea.

A most important thing to remember at the menstrual period is cleanliness. The external parts of the generative organs should at all times be kept scrupulously clean, but especially at the time of the menstrual flow, by the frequent use of warm water and soap. There is a mistaken notion in the minds of many women that bathing at this period is harmful. A cold shower or a dip would indeed be a very bad thing but to bathe the parts from a hand basin with warm water and castile soap is not only not injurious but is essential to health and comfort.

Beauty and Popularity.

Besides fitting you more effectively for your life's work, good health will incidentally increase and preserve your beauty and attractiveness. True beauty comes from within: it cannot be put on from without. Any make-up is like a false face, easily detected. Good health gives beauty, and a beauty that will last. Its foundation is health of mind and of body. Its expression is a sparkling, brilliant eye, a clear complexion, beautiful tresses, a graceful body and an active brain. Every girl and woman wants to be popular with her associates and if she has the beauty of personality she will always shine where ever she casts her lot. Today the girl is popular who glows with life, who can swim, dance, play out-door games and excels; who has plenty of energy for fun, and for endurance and when she has finished her daily tasks her pleasures do not tire her body. Good health produces high spirits, vitality, cheerfulness and leadership, and will help mightily to make you popular. Every girl likes to enjoy herself and to help afford enjoyment for others. She likes to attend parties, picnics, dances, and games in which athletic sports enter, for in these the healthy find the real joys of living. Physical fitness, by enlarging your opportunities for enjoyment and your power to help others enjoy, makes more such occasions possible.

How May The Girl Acquire Physical Fitness?

The rules of physical development are the simple rules of every day life. Those who would achieve the maximum vigor must observe at least five essentials.

1. Sufficient exercise of the right kind.
2. Sleep in fresh air, work in fresh air, and live in fresh air.
3. Get sufficient sleep—at least 8 hours a day, if young in age there may be required 8½ or 9½ hours a day.
4. Eat wisely, the proper kind of food and chew properly.
5. Chastity. Cleanliness of body and of mind.

Plenty of exercise, fresh air, sufficient sleep, three well-balanced meals a day, correct posture, and comfortable clothing will help to make you strong and well.

Exercise.

To keep physically fit, exercise regularly taken is necessary, and it must be taken every day of the year. Walking is the best of gentle exercise. 'Hiking' adds to its charm when it is in good company. Skating, canoeing, swimming, and games requiring running like handball or basket ball are excellent forms of outdoor exercise. Tennis is a splendid game for girls and develops habits of sportsmanship, stimulating body and mind and is an enjoyable sport.

Exercise makes the blood flow to every part, taking nourishment to these parts and removing waste poisonous products. This gradually strengthens not only the parts exercised but all of the body and the mind. Muscles that would otherwise be weak and flabby become round and firm. Girls who sit indoors, in offices or factories, at home, or in the school room, are using but a small part of their bodies. They need to make special efforts to exercise the unused muscles during their leisure hours.

Fresh Air and Sleep.

Always work in well ventilated rooms. Ventilation is an essential of health. We can go without water for days but air is an essential of life and we can go without it but a very few moments.

No room is large enough to sleep in if the windows are not open. Always sleep in a room with the windows open. Night air is not dangerous. It is the insect pests that prowl in the night that make night air bad. Screen your open windows to prevent the entrance of bugs, beetles, moths and mosquitoes. Spend considerable time each day in the open fresh air. Fresh air can be secured without much effort if you choose to find the way.

Sleep rests the brain and body by relaxing the muscles. A growing girl needs more rest than a matured woman.

Bathing.

Impurities from within are cast off through the pores of the skin. Keep these pores open. Stimulate your skin to action and you will have healthy colorful beautiful skin. Never be afraid of warm water and soap. Frequent bathing is necessary for health. The best way to bathe is to take a warm bath followed by a cold shower or sponge off then with a coarse towel rub the skin briskly. A cold bath is excellent for the girl except during the menstrual period. The rub down leaves the body warm and glowing and is followed by a feeling of comfort and well-being.

What a Girl Should Eat to keep Healthy?

A vigorous healthy body demands wholesome food eaten regularly and properly. Chew your food well and eat slowly enough to have your food well mixed with the digestive juices. Never bolt or wash down your bites with copious draughts of water or other beverage. Three meals a day are sufficient and eating between meals is bad for one's digestion.

The food taken should include fruits, vegetables, —fresh or canned—cereals including bread, especially whole wheat and rough corn bread, butter, eggs, and milk. A moderate amount of desert preferably of the simple kind. Meat once a day is sufficient.

Water needs to be taken freely—at least 6 to 8 glasses a day and if taken properly at meal time it aids digestion.

Removal of Body Wastes.

Nothing poisons the body and mind worse than retained waste material. The bowels and kidneys have a positive physiological function to perform the chief one is to remove waste. These can be aided in their work or may be seriously hindered by inattention. Hindrance leads to retention of wastes which with time break down health and impair physical vigor. Waste material in the bowels if not removed, generates poisons which may damage the entire system: destroy vigor and energy and promote sluggishness of both body and mind.

A healthy body requires that the bowels act at least once every day. The water (urine) as a rule gives but slight inconvenience and so comment is unnecessary.

Do not form the habit of taking drugs for the relief of costiveness but acquire the habit of regularity of bowel action by habituating yourself and so eating as to aid nature in this work.

Posture.

Not only unattractiveness but physical discomfort is occasioned by improper or incorrect posture of the body. Headaches, muscular pains, and disturbances of digestive organs as well as of the breathing apparatus is occasioned by improper posture, especially slouching positions which crowd the lungs and compress the abdominal contents.

The essentials of a good standing position are to "stand tall", chest up, not out,—the back touching an imaginary straight line. (vertical). The feet should be front to rear parallel, the toes pointing directly forward. Aside from health, the erect girl who carries herself with ease and grace, inspires by her very appearance, the confidence of her friends, her teachers and her employers.

The position of sitting may be similarly commented upon as here a correct posture is as essential to health as the standing posture.

Clothing.

Wear what is becoming. Do not trust to your own taste which may be off color but confirm your ideas by the opinions of others. Every style of beauty is improved by a color which harmonizes well. Never appear in extreme fashions unless conspicuousness is desired as at a fancy dress ball or in theatricals. Street and workday costumes should conform to prevailing customs and fashions. Never wear social dress to business. A low neck behind a counter or at a desk is as much out of place as high heel shoes and thin hose. Dress with becoming modesty.

Clothes should be loose-fitting, warm, light, and should hang from the shoulders, which have a bony frame and are well able to carry weight with out unduly compressing vital internal organs. Avoid the extremes of fashion in shoes and hats. For street wear and in places of employment low heels will prove not only attractive but practical and comfortable. The body needs a level foundation upon which to stand.

Glands and Their Functions.

Important in maintaining health in carrying on the work of the body are several organs of different sizes called glands. Each of these glands produce a special kind of secretion or juice. The largest gland in the body is the liver, which secretes bile (gall) a secretion which aids digestion and in excess or in disease causes yellowness of the skin (jaundice). Smaller glands in the cheeks and under the tongue secrete saliva (spit) which is an aid to digestion as well as lubricating the food while in the mouth to aid swallowing. Tear glands give off tears which moisten and cleanse the eye ball.

There are other glands, which instead of pouring secretions out where they can be seen send their product directly into the blood for certain definite purposes of physiological functioning. These glands are called the ductless glands and the functions are still enveloped in mystery. Of late however considerable scientific study has been given these glands and much has been learned of their purposes. The tonsils in the throat, the thyroid in the neck, and other similar glands are of this type. They are known as blind glands. The secretion of these glands play an important part in development.

Other important blind glands are the testes in man and the ovaries in woman. These glands belong to the sex or reproductive organs. The secretion from the ovaries is absorbed into the blood and carried to all parts of the body. This secretion causes woman's breasts to enlarge and her figure to develop, adding lustre to the hair and sparkle to the eye. It makes the brain clear and active. In short these glands when functioning normally change the awkward girl of 12 to 14 years into a bright attractive little woman. The secretion from these glands gives tone to the flesh and muscles and vitality to the nerves. This secretion is essential for the development of a normal girl

The Working Girl.

Necessity knows no law and when the family income must be aided and daughters must 'go out', the menaces to these children must be given consideration.

In another pamphlet we have touched upon the dangers to those who are 'stage struck' or who seek 'gay life'.

Here we desire to urge the community to build programs for the protection of the little miss who should have equal rights and yet in seeking them exposes herself to snares that would engulf her if left to her own devices. The working girl needs protection. The morally endangered and the waywardly inclined girls are to be found in every community and will ever, no doubt, be one of our most perplexing problems. More fated than her brothers to suffer from dangers of a sex nature, the perils and plights to which a daughter is especially exposed, touch as a rule the business side of her life.

The working girl is seldom responsible as the aggressor in her early acquaintance with depravity. She unfortunately is the passive victim of unfavorable surroundings and the outer forces of evil. Upon her, in her youth and ignorance and helplessness, are visited the tragedies which seem to run forever through the ages.

Young girls will continue to grow up with low moral standards, just as long as they are reared by unfit parents, among harmful home surroundings: they will continue lax in manner and conduct just as long as their ideals and habits are shaped by undesirable companionships: they will continue to venture into paths that are slippery just as long as it is human to crave attention and excitement: they will continue to stumble into pitfalls just as long as adolescent instability deprives them of judgment and the ordinary means of self-defense. Girls will continue to be despoiled and corrupted as long as vicious men and women lurk and scheme to exploit those who are unprotected.

It is from the ranks of the innocent, the inexperienced, the uninformed girls that scores and hundreds of recruits are each year drawn into the ranks of prostitution.

Because of these back-grounds which cause many of our young business women to fall by the way and depart from the path of morality we desire to give particular consideration here to some of the causes, which we think are preventable.

It is within the power of each community to lessen the powers and opportunities of these undermining forces. The challenge goes forth for each community to develop and maintain well-coordinated campaigns of both prevention and restoration.

The essentials for this work are:—
1. Alert community interest.
2. Protection against family neglect.
3. Check incipient waywardness.
4. Voluntary women protective officers.
5. Supervision of Social life.
6. Supervision of housing.

Quickening higher sentiments through religious nurture will ever be one of the mainsprings of right conduct.

Sex instruction must be given tactful consideration by parents that girls confronted with dangers may be forewarned.

Prosecute vigorously adult offenders against all girls.

Most communities have been too prone to attack the problem indifferently. However in view of the magnitude and seriousness of the problem of the girl who is exposed through her work may we not hope that citizens and officials will realize their duties and give intensive thought to a comprehensive program? This and this alone can discharge our duty whether it be humane or social or civic.

What a Young Girl Should be Plainly told when Entering Womanhood.

The honor and virtue of a girl is so precious that it behooves her to be constantly on her guard. Unfortunately due to a false modesty or lack of knowledge of how to impart information it is the almost invariable custom not to tell a girl in plain words what should be guarded against.

We desire here to briefly explain the methods commonly used by procurers—styled "Cadets"—men who make a business of getting recruits, girls for houses of prostitution or the pleasure of men who are willing to pay for such service. These men have also been termed "White Slavers" and they hang about places where young women are likely to gather—dance halls of the public variety, the 'movies,' and in shops and business establishments where a number of young women are employed. These devilish creatures have been detected plying their trade in the neighborhood of high schools and young women's colleges. Here they strike up or as they phrase it 'cut in' on conversation by taking up a common topic of the day in order to make an acquaintance. This accomplished, he ingratiates himself into the young woman's confidence, by giving her presents, automobile rides, and escorting her to different places —usually where her parents do not want her to go —cabaret dancing, and trips to nearby houses where parties get unconventional and at times pretty fast. Here they eventually drug her with knock-out drops, or drugged candies, or freely ply alcoholic beverages until the girl loses her self control.

Girls that are fond of pretty clothes, and of "good times" fall easy victims to these seducers. Some of these men have even gone so far as to pay courtship and propose marriage. Sooner or later some slumming party or auto ride is suggested, at the finish of which the girl finds herself a prisoner in some bawdy house with her clothing missing. She is closely guarded and communication with friends is impossible until the girl's spirit is broken and she is made to appreciate how great is her disgrace, after which she will not care to make her condition known to any one at home.

Many methods are used by White Slavers to make a victim tractable after they get them in their clutches. Personal violence is often used if persuasion is ineffective, and many of these girls confess to having been given a beating with a black eye to make them give in and succumb to the needs of the "cadet." A high spirited girl who makes a good fight is often rendered unconscious either through the use of drugs or drinks which have been drugged, and later awakening in a position which will so thoroughly disgust her with herself, she will not care what happens afterward.

Girls Traveling Alone should never get "Chummy" with Strangers.

There is a dangerous type of White Slaver, usually a benevolent appearing woman of middle age who makes it a practice to frequent railway stations in large towns and cities and 'pick-up' any young girl or woman who appears to be unaccustomed to traveling or who may have missed her way. These women some times travel between cities and pick up young women, especially when large colleges are assembling or dismissing their young lady pupils. One instance is recorded where one of these women actually entered one of our large schools for young ladies and tried to make converts. Fortunately she was detected before causing the ruin of several young ladies who had asked parental permission to leave school and take up theatrical art under her guidance.

When traveling it is well for young ladies to keep up the best composure and never let anyone, know your destination, especially if you are seeking employment as these men and women procurers will use any plausible excuse to get you to go with them. Decline all these invitations, there is usually a motive in quickly made effusive friendships. If you must travel alone to a large city the Travelers Aid will assist you and this savior of young women, has booths in nearly all railway stations or the ticket clerk will inform you where the nearest one may be found. Refuse all other offers.

Automobile "He-Vamps" and Taxi Driver White Slavers.

Two persons going in the same direction, one walking and the other motoring, it looks very natural to offer the pedestrian a lift, but be on your guard. Danger lies ahead if you accept.

Always refuse rides with auto "he-vamps" who pull up to the curb and smilingly invite you to get in and take a ride. Such rides usually cost a whole lot more than they are worth. Thousands of nice girls have lost honor and self-respect as a result of a 'joy' ride with a male stranger.

If the free auto ride giver was any good, he would not have to seek companions on the streets. If you accept his ride, ten to one he will have a "break down" in some lonely spot that suits his purpose, or, he will demand a payment, not in money, the alternative of which will be a long walk home. These despoilers who pick up girls on the street usually have a favorite road house where your cries for help would avail you nothing if you were attacked.

Investigations have proven that many taxi drivers are white slavers and often if not engaged in the practice of procuring, rent the use of their machines for despoiling young girls. When you have occasion to use a taxi be sure that it is the vehicle of a reliable concern and always insist upon riding in streets that are frequented and avoid using park roadways especially at night.

Advice for Girls Entering Womanhood.

You are in your 'teens' and are approaching maturity. Your body has undergone changes that are mystifying and you are curious. Nature is preparing your body for the sacred duties of Motherhood, just as it did for your mother.

Your menses have become established and they appear with luna like regularity. Should they disturb you, seek advice of your mother. Silly, false modesty may cause permanent ill health for you if you do not observe the natural rules of hygiene at these periods.

Avoid getting wet or chilled during your period.

Tight shoes are painful and affect your gait and alter your posture and make menstruation some times painful. High heels displace the generative organs of the female and cause muscle strain accompanied by pain.

Do not allow any boy or man to fondle, hug or kiss you. It is not lady-like and is dangerous. Boys that you allow such personal privileges often boast when with companions of what an "Easy Mark" you are. They frequently add to their remarks additional facts which may be untrue. Save your kisses for the fine fellow you will marry some day and then you will have no fears or vain regrets.

Many young men are veritable 'kissing bugs' and transmit many vile skin eruptions and venereal diseases by kissing promiscuously.

If you are away from home, never use a toilet article that is not your own. Always cover public toilet seats with paper before using them or else you may contract some unpleasant disease or vermin.

Babies grow within the mother's body—babies are not brought by the stork nor in the doctor's black bag. Your ovaries supply the seed that causes a baby to grow when it is brought into contact with the sperm cells of the male. This phenomenon of nature is possible at any time after menstruations have begun. If you need information or advice consult your mother and talk like a pal or not having a mother seek your physician or the health nurse. Don't look for information in patent medicine books, almanacs, or the advertisement of quacks.

Should You Teach Your Child?

There is a surprising amount of ignorance and mis-information on the subject of sex and sex diseases.

In these swift care free modern days a young girl who wishes to retain her purity will find it a constant battle. Her path is frequently beset with dangers and traps of all varieties to make her a thing unclean. The best rule is to obey society's conventions and have nothing to do with strangers. Be sure of those men or women you accept as friends. Stay away from questionable resorts, especially dance halls and cabarets. If you do these simple things you will have little trouble to keep that which is dearer to a woman than life itself —your virtue.

The prostitutes prayer: "O God deliver me from this bondage."

The Clandestine Prostitute. The girl of "easy virtue."

There is a class of young women who lead a life of shame by selling their charms for other things than money. Girls who sell their charms for money are titled by that ugly appellation "Whore or Prostitute." Girls who sport with men and consort with them outside of marriage are known as 'Snaps.' Maidens who have been betrayed and whose virtue is easy are as a rule unfortunate young women who are defectives mentally, in other words, near lunatics. No well-balanced woman will give herself up to a life of shame and disgrace voluntarily. Coarseness and vulgarity is naturally repugnant to all womankind. More so it may be stated, than to men. Every intelligent person knows that illicit sexual intercourse means a diseased body. No one in her mind could possibly become a prostitute. Men patronizing such places do so under cover of darkness and in the late hours of the night, so low down are they. Men who patronize prostitutes refuse to be recognized or greeted by a prostitute should they come together in a public place in broad daylight.

No prostitute will admit that she is diseased. One woman once took a vow to spread disease to a thousand men in revenge for one man who infected her.

The false pretense of passion a prostitute gives to keep your trade is just what she gave some other fellow a few moments before your arrival and she will give to some other poor fool who follows you. No prostitute will decline this illicit trade regardless of color or race, if her price is paid.

No matter how earnestly a prostitute assures you that she is free from disease, pay no attention to her. Nearly all of them are professional liars, or are drug fiends and drunkards.

If you must have companionship find a fine healthy girl and marry her. That's the only safe way.

Thousands of persons have acted on the mistaken belief that sex relations are necessary to health, only to find that through such indulgences they have impaired their health by contracting serious venereal infection. Many have thought that gonorrhoea, was "no worse than a cold." A list of the superstitions and untruths that daily pass muster owing to ignorance of sex is a terrible indictment of our modern prudery and false modesty.

Much has been done by our public health authorities and by physicians to remedy this ignorance but there is still considerable to be done before this blight to the happiness of hundreds of thousands of persons, especially women and children, may be destroyed.

The most important preventive against later vice and venereal disease is the proper education of the children with regard to sex. Your part, as parent is then to instruct your own boy and girl. You cannot evade this responsibility. It is not a matter for the public school, nor for the church, nor for instruction in groups but it is strictly a home and a parent problem.

Evidence of the Need For Sex Information.

Do you think that while the neighbor's children may need some such information, your own children will never have any such need?

It is not natural for children to be uninterested in the renewal of life which they see about them. Only an abnormal child, a dull child, a feeble minded child, fails to be curious about such things.

If your child remains silent about these matters or fails to ask questions, it is safe to conclude that this information is being obtained from other people. If you have dodged your child's questions about these matters, you can rest assured that these same questions are asked and answered from sources of which you would be ashamed.

Do you think that children with abnormal surroundings—the children seen in courts, jails, detention homes, reformatory institutions—are the only ones in need of sex instruction?

A large majority of boys get their first sex information from improper sources before the age of twelve years.

The ideas received from these improper sources have often led to some form of sexual practice.

Instruction in the past, when given at all, has been about 5 to 6 years too late. When given by the parent it has been crude and meagre. Public health officials are constantly coming in touch with boys and girls the victims of vice and disease and some of the cases appearing at the venereal clinics are mere children of the tenderest years.

FACTS ABOUT MARRIAGE

Every Young Man & Woman
SHOULD KNOW

Prepared by
S. DANA HUBBARD, M.D.
NEW YORK

Attending Dermatologist to the
New York City Children's Hospital
Dermatologist Letchworth Village
Director
Bureau Public Health Education, New York City
Department of Health

SEX FACTS FOR THE YOUNG MAN AND WOMAN ABOUT TO MARRY.

The Highest Wisdom.

"The great majority of people believe that all which is difficult to understand is immature, vague, and often false. The highest wisdom is simple, clear and goes through the brain straight into the heart."

Marriage: A subject sure to engross the attention of all normal young persons whether male or female. These will consider the likelihood of their own marriage and speculate as to why people enter into this bond.

"Of all the fabrics of society, marriage is the most complicated, the most delicate and the most significant."

Families require support and every contractor in this relation must be expected to give evidence of his ability as a provider before being allowed to take a wife. Marriage has always been regarded as normal and necessary. The Mohammedans considered it a duty and the Hebrews a religious duty. In Egypt it is considered disreputable not to marry. The Fijians believe that the unmarried do not get to heaven but that their souls are smashed to atoms. The purchase of a wife was the old practice though to day it is not indulged in this land.

Marriage embraces more than physical love, it involves constant companionship, mutual respect, and the welding of two individuals as one in thoughts, sympathies, aims, and purposes, blending their lives in love and sacrifice for their little ones.

Marriage naturally implies motherhood. There is no nobler word in any language than MOTHER. The young mother with her first born is a picture of joy and accomplishment that fills us with wonder and approbation. If there is a perfect home atmosphere—"the rallying place of affections"—every one does the utmost to make this place the happiest on earth.

There is a definite physical side to marriage, and if all husbands and wives were experts in gentleness and kindness the world would be spared many tragedies.

Maternity neither dims nor diminishes the energy, nor the intellectual faculties of the mother. On the contrary it acts positively on the virtues necessary for a proper membership in human society.

"Marriage is the beginning and the summit of all earthly civilization."

The union of a young man and woman in the holy tie of matrimony is the most important step in life. The entire future of both depends upon whether this step is taken seriously and after proper contemplation, because success and happiness depends upon wise selection. Marriage carries with it responsibilities far greater than the average person realizes.

Some marry for a home, some marry for money, some for position, some simply because it is fashionable. Foolish people. The person that marries for money, as the wag says humorously, earns it often times before he gets it.

Marriage should be only for love. Happy married life must be built upon mutual trust and devotion, not forgetting that there will be both happiness and trial and that come what may it is a case of mutual sacrifice and helpfulness.

No undertaking in life should cause more careful consideration and if ever an undertaking which affects both health and is worthy of seeking advice and the opinion of others' happiness nothing should be overlooked in making this step.

The man a woman should marry should be healthy, clean minded and strong, not a weakling —because the husband will be the father of the children and the offspring inherit mental and physical traits of the parents. Don't help perpetuate bad traits and bad character. You cannot go against nature in heredity.

Don't marry a man who cannot provide you with a home. Insist upon your own home, be it ever so humble a beginning. "Tall oaks from acorns grow." Boarding with either your or his family is unwise. Living in furnished rooms may ruin your life or his.

While it is a delicate subject for a woman to discuss, yet the matter of children is often times a stumbling block. Don't marry a man who does not want children, such a man will not want you very long. If he loves and loves truly, he will be eager to be the father of your babies.

In contemplating marriage, health is the first consideration. Have a careful understanding on this point. Insist upon both yourself and himself undergoing a careful medical examination to ascertain your fitness for marriage and parenthood. Never take this for granted. If too delicate for you to undertake have your parent or guardian do so for you. This test is for your protection, because many men "sowing wild oats" before marriage contract disease and so very few of them have their disease cured. If you do not insist upon this test you may some day find yourself with out children, or else the mother of weak, puny, diseased children.

If you are averse to having children, don't marry. You will be committing a sin that Nature will punish you for as surely as God exists. The world holds no more cowardly murderers than those who are involved in committing abortions to prevent child birth.

Do not allow your fiance any liberties with your person before marriage. He may be only testing you to learn if he can have them, but many engagements are ruined by this foolish mistake. Most men figure that if one man can have liberties before marriage other men can have similar liberties after marriage. Confirmed libertines on many occasions have proposed marriage only to deceive and obtain special privileges and this is one of the surest methods of ruining women, especially young women.

If the man you are about to marry loves and respects you, he will not ask you to degrade yourself by being his prostitute before marriage. Should you not refuse, he will surely bring this up in your family bickerings and "twit" you about your weakness, that is if he will marry you after you have allowed him to ruin you.

It is the woman's right to name the wedding day—insist upon doing this. Have a confidential talk with your parents, especially your mother or some other married woman about the obligations of the marriage relation as it affects the wife or mother.

There may be instances when elopements or run-away marriages are advisable but outside of the romance these are dangerous occasions for both man and woman. The vast majority of such hasty unions turn out badly.

Be sure the marriage license is legal. That the person performing the ceremony is duly authorized. Don't take any one's word for these facts but make certain. Make them prove it. This is emphasized to save girls from being victimized by 'fake' marriages.

Never marry a chronic alcoholic, you never reform him. Never marry a drug addict. He will lower you to his level and you will never elevate him. Such experiments are failures from the first. If you decide to marry, do so, long engagements are not advisable. The engagement period is a strain on both man and woman. Extravigances that most people can ill afford are usual during this period and it is money wasted that would be most useful in your new home.

Arrange your wedding day according to your menstrual period. Ten days after or ten days before. This will save you some embarassment.

In marrying, make no reservations. If there are reservations it were best not to marry. Wait for the man you are willing to share not only your heart but all your worldly possessions.

Some Facts The Young Man About to Marry Should Know.

Don't think that because you have been out after dark, and have called on a few young ladies that you are sophisticated in the matter of love.

If you are contemplating marriage talk this matter over with your mother, or your married sister or some married woman friend. Marriage means so much more than the average person considers and it is well to have counsel on the eve of this important change in your life relationship.

Are you situated so that you can support a wife and later on babies? Is the woman of your choice a person of good character and health? Are you a man of character and health? Is your future wife free from physical defects?

It is assumed that you have chosen the woman who will be your wife and who will be the mother of your children and the sharer of your future joys and sorrows and you probably consider her nothing short of simple perfection. But let us rest and analyze this proposition.

Your children will be what you are, therefore these questions are of deep importance.

Are you physically and mentally strong and healthy and is the woman of your choice? To determine this beyond the possible chance of oversight have a careful physical examination of both made. Are both free from disease. Now don't be foolish and think this superflous. Your fiance's family may have passed down a taint or two and you do not desire to be a party to a continuance of this hereditary transmission.

In assuming the responsibilities of married life, you are making yourself responible for the whole future life of a trusting girl who gives you her all unreservedly. Are you willing to give as much?

How about those past indiscretions? Of course it was years and years ago. But is the matter cleared. Do you know. If not have a careful physical test made to see that you are perfectly healthy and that that 'old dose' has left no traces. Don't take it for granted.

On your wedding night, be tender, considerate, and appreciate that that little wife has had a day of excitement and nervous and physical strain. Your wife and you are alone. She is absolutely yours and for the first time is entirely in your power. At your mercy. If you shock or disgust her by precipitancy or over eagerness, or zeal, appreciate it may be the undoing of your wedded bliss and joy. You may regret it the balance of your life. The consummation of the marriage relation is a new experience to her. Do not shock her by indelicate treatment or you may make yourself forever repulsive to her.

You should know that in the sex organ of the woman (virgin) that there is usually a thin membrane called the hymen. This has to be stretched or broken through by the male organ in sexual intercourse before the union is completed. In many cases this hymen is absent. This does not indicate that the person is not a virgin. Frequently it is necessary to destroy this in treatment for menstrual disturbances. The stretching or rupturing of this membrane is painful and so the operation should be carefully and considerately performed. In some instances it is necessary to have a doctor correct the condition if the hymen does not yield naturally.

Sexual Congress After Marriage.

Newly married people are prone to over indulgence in the sexual act, little realizing the great injury they cause their nervous systems. It has been truly remarked time and again that men use their wives simply as prostitutes, allowing their passions to sway them to the detriment of the health of both man and woman.

The sexual act is only for the purpose of reproduction. Any violation of Nature's laws through abuse or excess will be punished. Practice continence in the married state, excessive indulgence is wicked.

Sexual intercourse may be indulged in only when the desire is mutual and not to simply gratify the whims of either one. Each should study the other and show tender consideration for the health and well being of the other. Husbands who enforce selfish and unreasonable demands on their wives are just plain brutes. Many wives learn to loathe and abhor their husbands as a result of these demands. Husbands must remember that a woman is of delicate vitality and her strength is not equal to his. To a woman, who does not desire it, the sexual act is torture. It fills her with disgust and wrecks her family life. When the sexual act is not mutual it is nothing more than masturbation and may be even more harmful. It is not advisable for husband and wife to abstain from sexual indulgence for very long periods but there are times when it is imperative to practice self restraint.

For a married man, as for a single one, unreasonable sexual indulgence means reduced energy. It is not hard to pick out the person addicted to excesses, be they what they may. A man's system shows quickly and plainly inroads on his strength. Continence means a life time of vigorous sexual power, excesses only a year or more. Make your choice. If you do not wish children you should not marry.

Rearing a Family.

If you did not intend to have a family neither of you should have considered marrying. , Marriage presumes a home and no home is complete without those angel steps which totter towards daddy or mother.

Contraception presumes the prevention of pregnancy or refusing to rear children. There is no safe contraceptive.

The world contains no more contemptible and cowardly murderers than those who for some reason or other wilfully avoid or prevent childbearing. All over the world are instances of physical wrecks of women who have ruined their health with strong drugs and preventives of pregnancy. It has been said that a man who murders for money is a gentleman compared to that man or woman who make themselves a party to murdering an unborn baby.

Physiologically the baby is alive from the moment of conception. Life begins with the junction of the sperm with the ova. There is no period when it is safe to abort and no period when an abortion is done that does not kill the infant whether it is an embryo or fully formed child.

Abortions are dangerous and life destroying. Surgeons under proper operating technique may perform such to save life but at best it is a capital and serious operation. Always dangerous.

The Mistakes of the Bride-groom.

Justice and right demands that a man should consider the woman's views on the sex relationship, and that a woman has a just grievance when her own sex nature is not considered. The law of marriage however urges—the contrary and a woman must comply with the wishes of her husband or she furnishes justifiable grounds for divorce in very many of our states.

Any attempt on the part of man to invade woman's self-ownership is in violation of a natural law outside of the marriage relation. This also is both moral and legal law.

Marriage relations preconceive mutual consent, but there may be instances where such may be with-held by the woman and to violate this principle inevitably kills love between husband and wife.

Argument in favor of the right or duty of woman to assert and maintain the sanctity of her sex nature should be based upon equity. An argument also in its favor is that of human love and affection. Marriage to be valid and justified must be based upon love. The sexual relations are pure only so long as they are based on this principle. Therefore, when even in marriage the principle of primal right of the woman is ignored and violated, love withers and dies and the reason and validity of the marriage relation disappears. Marriage commits suicide when it violates its fundamental reason for being.

In matters of love, man is a mere infant in arms, while his passion is stronger and less controlled than that of woman. His love nature is undeveloped and primitive when compared to woman's. In matters of the heart, man is but a mere amateur in which woman is the finished and accomplished master. Not because of any special experience which the woman may have, and the man may lack, but the distinction is fundamental. A girl of tender years is often a natural ʝut unconscious coquette and the boy of such age is still a child. Girls of tender age control their fathers with all the skill of women of years of experience. The girl when in her " 'Teens' " often knows more of the art of love and display of affection than males of twice her age.

A wise man once remarked, "To The Average man, love is nothing more than a mere plaything"—or words to that effect. Men are interested in affairs of culture, civics, serious matters indeed, constructive industry etc. The affairs of love are his relaxations. Passion is a little fire with which he toys and which every now and then flares up and consumes him. Man's passions are admittedly stronger than the average woman's, but man seldom admits his ability to control and master his passions. With woman the opposite is the case.

Love is perhaps a kind of revenge for that man who has for years made a woman his subself, a serf as it were. Today in many homes we see the master of the house act as if he were master of creation, and the woman, the humble wife tolerates this treatment as if her meal ticket were more desirable than her personal independence.

Marriage to man is the fulfillment of his love, the festivities over, he returns to his usual sphere and is relieved. To woman marriage is the culmination of her life and is but the beginning of a new life with more worlds to conquer. Woman can hope for but little understanding from men while present conditions persist, and man's nonperception of this only makes the domestic tragedy greater.

In the consideration of the differences of tⱨⱪo

sexes, attention was given to a deadly parallel between the capacities and abilities of men and women. This may here be continued in considering love. Women in nature are more primitive, intuitive, and more emotional and the great unconscious processes of nature lie nearer to her. With woman sex is a deep and sacred instinct, carrying with it a sense of natural purity. The average woman utterly fails to understand the ability of the average man to divorce sex relation from love, or man's willingness to undertake the sex-relationship without the presence of love. Woman know that men indulge the physical passion without feeling of affection and she fails to comprehend this because she finds no corresponding desire within herself.

On the other hand man is too apt to consider that woman's willingness to participate must spring from the same source as does his—he then attributes to her the same motives and thereby loses the characteristic viewpoint and motive of the woman.

Woman looks forward to married life as a continuation of the days of courtship and reasons that the closer relation of marriage will add to instead of detracting from the manifestations of tenderness. Man on the other hand looks upon marriage as 'settling down' and after the strenuous efforts of courtship thinks that 'love making' is some thing that may well be dispensed with after the days of the honeymoon. In this 'settling' the man often thinks that the sentimentalities of courtship is a thing of the past and can be dispensed with when matters are consummated by marriage.

Marriage to a man is like catching a street car, having caught it after a chase, the man sits down and comfortably enjoys himself by reading his paper and there is no occasion for further exertion when once the car has been caught.

The effect of the old notion, that of ownership of the body, of the wife by the husband has resulted in tragedies by the score. All of which might have been avoided were the man educated and informed regarding the natural rights of a woman, and her instinctive feelings on the sex relationship.

This deplorable ignorance is not so much the result of any special coarseness as it is the lack of proper education on the subject of love and marriage.

It would work a welcome revolution if mothers of boys and young men would bring themselves to the task of instructing their sons concerning the feelings and sentiments of young women regarding certain delicate relations of the married state. If this were done, these parents would add to the happiness of the woman who becomes the wife of her boy. This is work for women. Until women rise to this demand men will continue to fall far short of the ideals which women seek to find in them.

Mistakes of the Honeymoon.

The man entering marriage with his peculiar views often commits a grave offense against the spirit of love—against the person of his wife—at the very beginning of the relationship.

Many a young woman entering marriage has been so shocked, horrified and disgusted by the ignorance, brutality, and sensuality of man, that her love takes wings, never to return.

Every physician can relate instances of unbelievable grossness on the part of the otherwise considerate thoughtful and kind lover, on the occasion of the 'first night', not due to innate depravity of the groom but rather to lack of education on sex matters.

Many a man, in after years learning the truth has been mortified and grieved at heart when he remembers these experiences.

What the Young Husband Should Know.

The remedy for the above evil is simple indeed. In the first place, the young man should appreciate that his bride is exhausted from the preparations for the marriage and is in a state of high nervous excitement from the ceremony itself. Time is needed for adjustment to the changed conditions.

Courtship has awakened a feeling of confidence and love. Marriage properly consummated will awaken mutual confidence and lasting affection which may be blasted if these mistakes occur.

Many a husband has had cause to regret in his lack of consideration that he has allowed his passion to awaken in his wife feelings of disgust sufficient to blight love and quench all prospects of future happiness between them. He renders himself unhappy and his wife miserable. Ignorance, lack of consideration and passion had made a triumvirate which has destroyed the climax of this drama and another tragedy is recorded, the culmination of which is divorce.

It is indeed enough to bring color to the cheek to think of the scores of wives who almost daily confess to their physicians that they have been literally raped by their own husband and on the first day of their blessed conjugal relationship.

Young man, heed the injunction—"Don't be in too great haste to crush the bloom from the fruit you covet." Practice in lawful wedlock the arts of the experienced lover.

In woman, love throbs in every pulse, thrills in every fibre of her being: her life is love, she gives herself to the one she truly loves.

The confession of the 'ruined' girl is that she gave herself because she loved and trusted with her whole heart. Happy indeed is that union in which the man understands woman's nature.

The Immorality of The Marriage Relation.

"The deplorable lack of scientific education in the principles of sex, sex life, sex functioning and the sex relationship., to which we have often alluded is not confined strictly to young people out of wedlock, or those about to enter the same; it extends even to persons who have been married for years."

Many persons, men and women, enter marriage without understanding the incidents of parenthood or the fundamental physiological principles of sex.

Many persons, after living in marriage for many years, acquire information regarding sexual physiology, which if it had been known earlier, would have prevented suffering, pain, and sorrow.

Sex facts should be known to all married persons—they in our estimation should be known before not after marriage; but in our experience few indeed know even elemental facts.

One of the most glaring errors entertained by the average person is the belief that marriage throws the mantle of privilege, morality, and sanctity over all and any sex relationship between man and wife.

The average married couple, man and wife, are of the opinion that there can be no sexual immorality between husband and wife. Many hold the view that the marriage benediction automatically removes all moral obstacles and that once married all necessity for restraint, moderation or moral consideration in sex relations fade away when the notes of "the wedding march" sink into silence.

The voice of science refuses to admit that the ceremony of marriage nullifies the laws of nature. That physiology establishes not only the moral but the natural law. This being indicated by the expressions of 'instinct' in the lower species of animal life. They may commit a wrongful act, and not be held to account in the courts of law, yet nature inflicts her penalty and either the man or the woman pays, and not infrequently both do so.

It must be remembered that not all law is written, for the highest and most forceful law is that which is designated by man as "Un-written", and Nature's laws are of this class, and are firmly fixed, and as unalterable as are the season's change, the penalties likewise are invariably demanded and exacted.

To those who thus either in ignorance or willfully violate these relations the term immoral may be attached, for they not only often injure each other, or the one the other, but they bring suffering, pain and misery to other persons born and yet to be born.

Excessive sexual indulgences in marriage produce as lasting evil consequences as similar ef fects in the unmarried and in the opinion of tho impartial constitute legalized prostitution.

A man of great vital force, united to a woman of evenly balanced disposition, through misuse of marriage privilege may place his wife on the nervous sickly list or vice versa. In the blindness of his or her animal nature, the law in this matter, is to acquiesce, though such fulfillment is with a heavy heart, for love is absent, the bestial nature having stifled this delicate sentiment by the ex pression of the lust of the stronger disposition.

There are women, strongly passionate, often diseased, (nyphomania, irritation of clitoris, etc.) with strong animal natures and in the exercise of their sex desires soon reduce the husband to a physical and mental standard just below that of the brute and long before the fulfillment of his just allotment of time on earth, his career is fore shortened by death, caused by exhaustion of his physical forces.

The honeymoon often is one nightly repetition of legalized prostitution sinking the pure, the high and holy into the low and debasting lust of over excited passion.

If you would have happiness and peace and strength grow in that new relation, exercise your will power to control your passion and let love divine guide you to marriage bliss and healthy parenthood.

It must be understood by men and women that the result of sex excesses is as disastrous to the mind and soul of the married individual as is un legalized prostitution.

THE EXPECTANT FATHER

The father of the new baby—the expectant father—has a greater duty and responsibility than paying the doctor's, nurse's, druggist's bills and other incidental expenses. He should place himself in good health before his wife becomes pregnant. He should, if perchance infected with one of the social diseases at any time, be sure he is cured before conception takes place. He should be companionable, and make allowances if his wife is peevish, irritable, highstrung or nervous; under similar circumstances he would be quite as bad, probably worse; he should be kind, indulgent and forgiving; whether his wife is right or wrong, she is always right and he is always wrong—during pregnancy; he should encourage and soothe her and help her look on the bright side of things; he should be interested in the coming event, and talk of the future in a spirit of hope and happiness; he should share half the burden and responsibility of parenthood; he should check his business troubles before he enters the home. As he has half the responsibility in the creation of infant life, he should share at least half the responsibility for the future well-being of the baby after its birth.

THE BUSINESS OF BEING A FATHER.

Why is it that men, as parents, should regard the daily world of business activity as more important than the world of their domestic life?

In the world of home is involved all the future of the family and we might safely add, that of the Nation.

The home demands the best abilities that lie in a man.

The art of being a father involves not only heart and affection but brains, the best intelligence is demanded. A man gives that to his business because business demands that much. Man thinks about his business. He thinks about the people with whom he does business. He considers the qualities and characteristics of his associates in the business world. He is concerned with his contemporaries and his competitiors as well as with his individual customers. But in the home the business of being a father often times finds at the head of the family a man bankrupt in ideas, thoughts, or consideration, for the home and its occupants. To have the members of the home bring results, or attain success in life, some one must direct, otherwise definite performances with definite results will run askew and result in failure.

All of us at times think over our acts and retrospectively compare our acts with those of another. Consider the following and compare your consideration of your home folks:—Theodore Roosevelt, the conspicuous American, and busy man of affairs, great affairs—often times affairs of the nation—with full days, numberless engagements constantly pressed by persons and yet in the midst of this complicated and difficult activity found time some how to write to his children and the members of his family. He took time to interest himself in their affairs and give them his best mind and the frequent expressions of practical advice from his host of varied experiences tempered with the affections of his great heart. Can you not do as much?

> The writer has a family and has always lead a busy life, day in and day out. In thirty years of public service he has never lost a day from his labors and with it all, he has always been reasonably close to his home affairs. His relationship to the members of the home he views with more than normal fatherly interest. He is at all times in reasonably close touch with his home, either by telephone, letter or even postal card. Never leaving home without announcing his departure and his destination and expected time of return, never returning without seeking the presence of the home members and taking up the thread where he left off. As a father he has a passionate desire that his children should be educated, well guarded, and given a fair opportunity for development and self-expression in study and work.

If occasion requires his absence for more than a day from home the daily touch is kept by exchange of letters. These letters build a chain of mutual confidence and helpfulness one toward the other.

Too many men take it for granted that the morning means departure for business, that the members of the home know about it and that is sufficient. The evening of course brings father home, dinner is served and then it is out or to bed. Father must not be annoyed by wife or children as he is the tired business man. A daily monotony that is nerve disturbing.

How changed is the atmosphere when pets and children vie to say the last good bye and on the return all eyes and thoughts are on "dad's return and there's a race to have the first "Hello Dad."

These cheerful greetings are not the spontaneous welcome of mother or child who wants some thing but are the result of daily evolution in love and honor. Happy indeed the father who builds such a home. Great is the loss to those who do not.

The Un-married Father.

In attempting to estimate the social consequences of illegitimacy we must consider briefly the unmarried father.

Men in this category belong as a rule to the vagrant group. Often times but little is known of their type or the causes which bring them into being.

One must realize however that the unmarried father suffers though to a less degree from the same public disapprobation than falls upon the mother of an illegitimate child.

There is no doubt that the father frequently finds it hard to live down the result of his misbehaviour, for it also becomes difficult for him to form latter a union with a decent woman who knows of his previous misconduct and of others he is inclined to be very chary and skeptical. Should his irregularity be secret he is in more or less constant fear less the discovery of his irregularity be made known to further embarrass and annoy him.

When the unmarried father is already married, the birth of a child by a woman not his wife is attended by consequences that are obviously serious. One must say, however, that the parent is not here subjected to criticism by those with whom he comes in contact who are familiar with his action, but the unmarried father is open to the same stabilizing influences which the bearing of an illegitimate child frequently produces upon the mother.

We have known men who have grown away from reckless indulgence by the supporting fact of parenthood, and who have done their utmost to educate their children in a way by no means unworthy. No matter how much we may say against the injustice of a state of affairs which enables the father frequently to escape the consequences of his act, leaving the woman or girl to bear the preponderant burden, the causes of this seemingly uneven distribution of justice lie in the nature of things themselves, namely, in the obvious fact that it is the woman who bears the child.

It is however patent that the frequency with which the father escapes censure or responsibility is increased by the existing double standard of morals, because society tacitly assumes that the sex instinct in men, being less complex and less fraught with inhibition should normally find more direct expression.

There is indeed a need for careful study of the unmarried father and there is no limit to the material if it be sought and exposed.

Suffice it to say, that the unmarried father does not always escape and that a mess is not always cleared by additional exposures but the placing of responsibility and the squaring of the financial obligations here as a rule satisfies society and the further embarrassing relationship is relegated to oblivion and not to publicity and social study, the best for all.

DR. HUBBARD'S SEX FACTS

In our efforts however to raise the moral standard and do away with a double standard of morals this matter must be considered somewhat differently than it has heretofore been considered and disposed of by both courts of justice and society generally.

To deter and prevent these embarrassments society must erect standards of social conduct where man will be placed exactly on the same plane as that of woman under these circumstances and social disapproval measured and charged equally upon both sexes. Whether the results of such action will invariably prove beneficent or not is an entirely different question.

Why Girls Are the Home Makers.

Men have always demanded that the woman whom they marry be pure. Girls and women have a special work to do therefore in helping to build up a high standard of sex conduct. They must demand clean living of the men with whom they associate. Frank, wholesome companionship on the part of the girl or woman will encourage the same sort of companionship from the man or boy. Good manners are born of respect for one's self and for others. A handshake extends a warm friendly greeting. A kiss should mark the pledge of love. A girl who does not value these expressions highly and does not use them sparingly makes herself cheap, common and vulgar. She weakens her power of self-protection and makes herself a mark for men to mar, and in this loose conduct, indicated by familiarity, usually succeeds. If the woman really regards man's respect she will not seek to win it through acts and words of familiarity, nor will she wear clothing which tends to arouse sex desires. Physical attraction alone will never wholly satisfy: lasting love and friendship are of the mind as well as of the body. Their foundation is mutual respect and understanding and their highest expression is a deeply spiritual emotion. A girl's success and happiness will depend largely upon her choice of associates and finally upon her choice of a husband. Because she will choose her husband from her friends. It is important that her friendships be based upon qualities that will wear. Hasty marriages, following an acquaintance of only a few days or weeks often result in unhappiness because they are not founded on a love based upon a knowledge of each other. Fit partners for life are those who understand and respect each other's views, who recognize each other's faults as well as their virtues and who are willing to work together for lasting companionship.

A true home-maker shares her husband's responsibilities, enters into the lives of her children and of her community. By developing her own mind and spirit she is able to give the best of herself. She draws the best from others, and her husband and her children love her and work for her gladly.

The men and women of today can determine in a large degree the kind of women and men who will make up the world of tomorrow.

A girl can, by keeping herself fit and by marrying a man who is physically fit, give her children a clean bill of health. Fineness of character on a fine physical foundation gained from healthy parents will exert a wholesome and splendid effect on the home of the family of the future.

ft is the woman who is peculiarly the home-maker. She can determine whether her home is to be a place where people simply eat and sleep or where her family and friends will find inspiration, comfort and health habits in sympathetic companionship.

The opportunities for woman's development and her ability to contribute toward the creation of a better world were never greater. At last all activities are open to her. She will play an active and interesting part in the world's work. Whatever that part may be, it is essential to have good health. Women of pioneer days possessed clear minds and vigorous bodies which enabled them to produce a hardy race and their record is a challenge to you. Only as you are similarly qualified can you in your home and in your community meet this challenge of a glorious past by your achievements.

AN UN-ANSWERABLE ARGUMENT.

A young Girl must know SOME-TIME about herself, then why not select the time to teach her these necessary sex problems?

Recently there was published a very good book, which relates to this subject—it is "A Young Girl's Diary"—and here are found in splendid sequence the expressions of a young girl who seeks to know some thing about herself. This book should be read by every mother and by all young ladies. It might not be unwise to help the young adolescent miss approaching puberty to read it understandingly.

To many of us who are interested in girls there is no doubt but that these little misses are kep' too much uninformed. In our opinion, "A Young Girl's Diary," expresses just the yearnings that have been indicated in my consulting room on a number of occasions by both girls and young women. To have these thoughts expressed for you in a refreshing wise manner makes this book an important one in this work.

Girls between the ages of eleven and thirteen, are neither children nor grown-ups. These present problems to parents, but when the family is a unit and there is that unselfishness and consideration for one another that is usual the girl just goes along under brother's and father's protection until her sweetheart comes along and then the psychological reaction is bewildering. Few girls are introspective—ponder over themselves —their thoughts as a rule are on their studies, their playmates, their dresses or other things, so that their young lives are crowded to full measure. However there are more of these introspective girls than adults are prone to believe, such consummate actors are they, that it is really difficult to pick out the little party who is beginning to 'sit up and take notice'.

As a father and as a family physician I think it is an awful mistake for any parent to make to let a girl go through the change of puberty without preparation. Girls must not simply drift into sex knowledge. Drifting never took any one to any definite place and if it did, it did not get there on time. To let girls get sex facts by listening to words dropped incautiously here and there by adults gives misinformation or the information is misinterpreted.

The waste of energy in the hours of "talking

about those things," in toilets, in bed before the lights are out, and in the presence of chance acquaintances bold enough to bring up these topics places the matter on a low ideal and destroys any spiritual significance in the sexual relationship. This natural curiosity of the young girl is a most potent argument for parents to meet this issue with first hand facts.

How many girls are 'wrecked' through ignorance of sex we have no means of ascertaining definitely by statistics but if it is considered that about 800 to 1000 girls leave home and mysteriously disappear in one large city every year and that of the number few are located after disappearance, the reason for such absconding has been almost invariably due to some sex matter.

Girls are naturally imaginative and are sensitive and respond to inherent beauty but if they be overwhelmed and seduced their reaction is not that of 'talking things over with mother' but to fear discovery and to hide their embarassment. So they take wings and fly. My friend if you have daughters, as I have, read "A Young Girl's Diary", and you'll find it is not a book of trivialities, and it may help you solve your daughter's problem.

When puberty approaches, anticipate it, by wholesome family conference or by selective reading on this subject. If unable to locate suitable literature through your library consult your health officer.

In-door Recreation for Girls.

There may be those who think dancing improper, and in some instances certain dances are improper.

When I was young the waltz and polka were taboo by the elder members of my family and the only time I could do "round" dances was without their knowledge. I did them and this was one of my earliest deceptions of my elders and considering the good times they afforded me, I cannot see that this dancing did any harm to any of my partners or myself.

Today physicians as well as physical directors both agree that dancing is a recreation of positive physical and mental benefit. Dancing affords quiet rhythmical exercise of the muscles, and relaxation to the mind. No other recreation is so beneficial and has less detrimental results. Dancing is primarily a recreation, a form of exercise in which certain faculties and muscles are pleasurably engaged while other faculties and muscles fatigued by normal labor are permitted to rest.

The general rule for recreation is that mental labor requires physical recreation and physical labor requires mental recreation: but the two forms of recreation can be combined if the tired faculties or muscles are not employed. When dancing is done in a well lighted hall properly ventilated and heated, to music of a good orchestra surrounded by congenial companions dancing is beneficial.

In our opinion, in the promoting of better understanding of the sex relations and improving the social atmosphere of our boy and girl in finding places of amusement, we cannot do better than by promoting dancing under proper supervision. We have of late years observed in the heated season how our "Block" parties helped bring together good boys and nice girls in the neighborhood of

DR. HUBBARD'S SEX FACTS

their homes. Another step in this direction would
be the formation of a girls' and boys' orchestra
and a dancing club in the neighborhood school
house. Dancing might be on Friday nights and
parents could have a weekly meeting which would
afford opportunity for chaperonage and also supervision of the young folks, it would develop a
love for music and afford opportunity for practice and the weekly dance would give splendid
opportunity for recreation and also a chance for
good boys to meet nice girls and vice versa.
Friends made in this way would be productive of
lasting social relationship which would be ben-
ficial for the home as well as the community.

The following reasons in favour of dancing are
therefore offered. Dancing is healthy. Dancing
promotes worthy home membership. Dancing
gives command of fundamental powers and processes. Dancing affords relaxation and recreation. Dancing affords a vocation. Dancing makes
good citizens. Dancing has an ethical value.

Dancing would bring about better relations between pupil and teacher. Dancing in the schools
should never be held if the two sexes are to be present without a teacher being present at all times.

One of the best and first influences noticed by
block parties and school and church club dances
was the drawing away of boys principally but
girls quite often from cabarets and public dance
halls. One youngster in replying to why he was
not so often seen at a certain cabaret, where he
had been a frequent attendant and was known
as a chronic dance hound, replied 'O! I have a
good time now at the club and I meet nicer girls
and besides it don't cost me nothing'.

These boys and girls must be given exercise and to get this in a pleasurable manner, nothing is better than dancing.

There is but one caution and that is about dress. This for both boy and girl must be simple, inexpensive, and decorous.

The Parents' Part.

The one deterring fear of sex discussion is that it may awaken sex consciousness, which is groundless if undertaken properly. The musician studies harmony and rhythm, and in such method must the study of sex be undertaken that there may be kindled an appreciation of the wonders of nature and a realization of the beauties of the process of reproduction because many a traveler goes unheedingly through life and misses that which would bring both pleasure and instruction.

For instance children in their innocence are unabashed at that which would discomfort adults, who may have acquired, through ignorance of these wonders, a sense of guilt or of shame. We should use every possible opportunity and endeavor to clear the mists as far as possible and substitute intelligent respect for the marvelous processes by which we were created.

The object of education is to make individuals fit for service to humanity and bring happiness to themselves and their children. Very young children ask endless questions, that being the way they learn in their primitive stage. They soon ask whence they came and where they go and as they grow older these apparently idle questions take on serious concern. It is instinct to want to know something of the origin of life. They should be given honest answers, the completeness of detail depending much on the age and understanding of the child. Leaving the question unsatisfied or falsified is simply postponement and an opportunity for helpfulness lost.

Ignorance is excusable in the young but not in the mature. Spiritual beauty of sex ideals cannot be inculcated by reading misleading advertising literature or mysterious pamphlets about sex. A physician gives information regarding sex matters with the same candor and directness that he discusses digestion or the circulation. There is no blush in nature in regard to sex. Imagine a rose embarrassed or butterflies blushing and ashamed of perpetuating their kind. Animals fulfill the requirements of their natures in season in a natural method. Sex has long remained to many persons a most mysterious problem. Marriage is as sacred as any of the sacraments. Teachers praise honor, justice, brotherly love and charity, then in truth's name why hesitate to lay stress on one of the highest social virtues? Let us forthwith eradicate the thought that the word "sex" is undignified and vulgar. Sex is the sum of the peculiarities of structure and function that distinguishes a male from a female organism. The essential attribute of the male is the sperm cell and of the female is the ova or egg.

The youth whether in field, factory, office, shop or home, needs help to solve the diffculties and perplexities concerning himself. The science of health is hygiene. To the right minded a study of sex should be ennobling and a stimulus to higher aims and endeavors.

The better the young man and young woman understand themselves and their functions the better they can adjust and control their desires and actions.

Sex instructions should begin when children are old enough to be interested in flowers and vegetables and pets. These also afford opportunity for observations on mating and on parentage. A child thus taught from observation of nature thinks of reproduction in an unselfconscious manner. Much depends upon the attitude of mind in the young individual. Here rests a great responsibility upon the wise and the mature. It is but human to make mistakes in life, so let the more intelligent encourage the unwise in ways of living, of working, and of home building and in rearing little ones that will lead to happiness and health and away from the morasses of disease and misery.

Self control must be cultivated in character. Unbridled selfishness will wreck humanity either upon the shoals of criminality or the rocks of disease. Vicious tendencies will creep in unless parents are always definitely cultivating high moral standards. Masculine virility needs to be blended with affection and feminine affection with devotion that through the coming together of the sexes in social relations mankind may be raised to greater spiritual heights.

Knowledge of sex facts imparted at the right time in the right way is a help to right conduct. A youth instructed in the fertilization of plants and reproduction of animals from early childhood will give no special thoughts to sex knowledge any more than he will to mathematics or history. Under ideal conditions the boy or girl trained as one should be trained in physiological functions would give sex no more consideration than he or she would to breathing.

It is only because this field is so often passed by on the other side that there is mystery and this secrecy begets curiosity.

Here is an opportunity to clear the wrongfulness of bird destruction in nesting season, of hunting deer or rabbits that are either bearing or nursing young. Judicious counsel will develop a natural respect for motherhood and parentage that may banish awkward embarassments later on in the lives of our children.

Parents' Responsibility for Imparting Sex Knowledge.

Sex education includes a study of the whole process of reproduction and the nurture of children, the meaning of marriage, what is meant by prostitution, the venereal diseases, illegitimacy, and the hygiene of recreation. These cannot be taught at any one time or in any one place better than in the home with the parent as teacher. The co-operation of churches, schools, the press, clubs, and societies is both necessary and helpful.

Your home is the natural place for satisfying the early curiosity of your children directing their adolescent energy and building up habits of self-control. All that other agencies can do to give your children a wholesome point of view will be nullified, if the parent fails to do his full duty in this respect.

Always Instruct the Child Before Puberty.

The parent's duty to the child is to see that coming events are appreciated. Puberty is an important change and a positive one. Puberty is the period when bodily sexual development is noticeable. **This** begins in girls at about eleven to thirteen years of age. In boys it begins a little later about thirteen to fifteen years.

As early as six years is none too soon to begin sex information. At this age the little one is an animated question mark, a walking riddle. Here is the very beginning of sex education. Curiosity at this age is instinct. It is natural. The myth of Santa Claus or St. Nicholas has just about been relegated to oblivion and the little one should be told the truth—because if you do not, then the playmates or school associates will undo your white lie and cause the little one much embarrassment—Answering the question satisfies curiosity. The essential fact to be borne in mind is that curiosity and interest are aroused by those things that the child does not know about, not those that he knows about.

All the questions will not be asked at once. Only the immediate question should be answered. Information given a little at a time will be absorbed a little at a time. It is the experience of trainers that reiteration is most essential in training. Questions from youngsters are a sign of a healthy attitude.

It is impossible to give an accurate schedule of just how this knowledge should be imparted in every case as children even at the same age differ most markedly. Surroundings of boys and girls vary widely so that no general rule may be aplied. The safest rule as to time to begin giving sex information is to be guided by your child's questions and if no questions are asked then bring up the topic a little at a time to plant correct in formation and displace the misinformation of pals, chums and playmates.

Questions and Answers. Samples of Childish Inquisition in Relation to Sex.

1. Who made me? Where did I come from? Where did the chickens come from? Where did the kittens come from? Are you mother to all of us?

Every one of these questions has been asked numberless times by our little inquisitors.

"Babies grow inside of their mother's bodies just as little rabbits in their wool covered home in the burrow. When their eyes can stand the light of day and their little naked bodies are covered with down and the sun shines bright old mother bunny brings them out for an airing. But if an enemy comes near, like the bad old hawk, she stamps her foot and the whole litter run to their snug little home dug way down under the ground.

2. How is the baby born? How does a hen have chickens? How did the baby calf come?

Every house has a gate and as from this gate there is a path to the house so there is a gate and path for the baby. This passage way opens at the lower part of the body. We should never touch that part of the body except to keep it clean or we harm it. (Boys should have this question answered and stress the point of how these blind glands promote vigor and health). (Girls should be warned against self-abuse).

3. Does it hurt to have the baby born? Why does the doctor come when baby is born?

Yes it hurts mother, but she is so happy to have a baby all her own that she soon forgets the pain.

The doctor comes to take care of the baby, because it is so tender and delicate. (Never emphasize the pains of labor in conversing with a child).

4. Can I tell my chum how our baby was born? He told me that the doctor brought babies in his black bag.

No. Some parents don't want to tell their children any thing about this and they never talk about such things. Never talk to any one about family matters without first asking mother. It is not nice.

5. What does it mean to be half collie and half bull pup?

This means that one parent was a collie dog and the other parent was a bull dog. All dogs have a father and a mother. Birds also have parents just as babies do. (This often satisfies childish curiosity).

There is a splendid opportunity, if such a question is asked by a boy or girl to arouse self-respect for reproduction and fortify their minds against vulgar talk and improper use of the sex organs. The explanation may be continued in practical form by showing how plants reproduce. For instance:—

"The seed is inside of the mother flower, but it does not grow into a new flower until the pollen dust has mixed with it. Every life begins with the mixing of two seeds. Every animal has a part of his or her body with tiny bits of seed which coming together start new lives. Some time as in the case of fish, the parts come together outside of the body, but in animals they mix in the mother's body, where they can be much better taken care of."

Thus it will be seen that it is simply a question of the parent knowing something of the scientific relations and passing this knowledge first hand to the offspring. If this is done then the advent of pets, excites no curiosity and along with it the arrival of a baby brother or sister is taken as a natural consequence of a happy and healthy home.

Indirect Training.

From 16 to 19 years of age our children, when no longer children nor yet full grown still require parental guidance more or less indirect.

Direct instruction should not be repeatedly given except as indicated, one simple thing at a time, one question answered and amplified by information that will satisfy the little questioner and not cause such thoughts to linger and arouse sex stimulation.

Keep your youth's mind off the sex question as much as possible but never shut him or her up and never evade your parental responsibilities.

At this age, the love of games and recreational activities will produce enthusiasms and interests which will diminish temptations to wrongful sex activity. Overlook no opportunity to encourage natural athletic interest. Also encourage eating wholesome food and keeping the bowels in good working order. See that the child gets an abundance of fresh air and exercise and from 8 to 10 hours sleep a day, every day in the week. Insist upon habits of frequent bathing and personal cleanliness.

While girls are not so universally enthusiastic for physical perfection at this period the parent should encourage as much as possible their physical development and participation in out of door sports.

Encourage the boy to make things, keep him busy. Do not give the boy red meat more than once a day. With the passing of childhood this is the time of times to develop high ideals and unselfish endeavor through literature.

In normal boy and girl life the developing sex life appears in an attraction for friends of the opposite sex. The manifestation known as "Puppy" love must be carefully guided and directed but it must not be suppressed. Encourage boys and girls to mingle socially at frequent intervals and particularly at places where adults can be present.

The practices of familiarities between the sexes known as spooning, petting parties, kissing games, presents a serious problem for the parent. It is positively useless to say "Don't do it." The real harm and the unfairness of such improper conduct should be pointed out clearly and directly. Evasion here is critical.

Where to Get Additional Sex Information.

Consult your physician.

Consult your health officer or your health nurse or your community clinic or club, where you will find well trained persons willing to aid you.

Consult your librarian and make known your wants and secure the right kind of literature and read it carefully.

Write to the American Social Hygiene Association of your State and they will try to serve you.

When impossible to get this from these sources consult your priest, your minister or your rabbi.

While advice is helpful, and literature informing

yet to bring this subject out of secrecy, mystery
and darkness, intelligent study is necessary for
the parent. It is most important for the parents to
do their part in instructing and directing their
boys and girls.

The "Dangerous" Age (?) of Woman. The 'Change of Life.'

In middle age—35 to 50—there occurs a change
in the menstrual activities of women. This is
physiological and natural. It denotes the end of
the child bearing period. At this period there are
often startling nervous affections and occasionally
these spend themselves in the manifestation of
strong sex impulses. They may occur unexpectedly
and without understanding on the part of the
woman, who has heretofore not experienced these
unusual impulses. This alteration may cause the
most astonishing change even approaching such
abnormal conditions as to approach loss of mental
balance. This has led medical men to character-
ize this period as "the dangerous age," and this
phenomenon is explained as the last effort on the
part of nature to have the woman play the part
of mother, the final 'flash' as it were of the reproduction instinct before it expires. These changes
particularly those mental are indeed serious and
the utmost care and nursing will be needed to
clear this climax successfully.

Sexual Indulgence During Menstruation.

Plain writing here is necessary, owing to the
fact, that among the ignorant it is tradition that
if a woman is without passion this is the time of
her life to arouse sex desire.

Although it is enough to make a man ashamed

of his sex, we must realize that these superstitions and beliefs must be openly combated by a denial.

The instinctive laws of cleanliness and delicacy should be ordinarily sufficient to restrain sexual appetite but in appreciation of true conditions in the world it is discovered that these are without influence under many conditions of marriage relationship.

Moses the Divine Law Giver of the Jews gave positive injunctions to his people and this race maintains their integrity in observance of Biblical commands.

Scientifically speaking indulgence of sex relations during menstruation is hazardous, as it may occasion bleeding, internal congestion, even inflammation of both male and female organs of generation, and many other illnesses. It is a well accepted opinion in medical circles that sexual congress during the menstrual period is fraught with many dangers. All marital relations should therefore be suspended during the menstrual period.

Sex Education in Relation to Public Instruction.

Heads of families, parents, guardians, and public officials should, in view of the prevalence of these diseases and their continued increase consider carefully the following questions and answer them in group form in a community. When a number of such questions are collected, an analysis should be made and carefully considered with general discussion that additional light may be shed on this question.

1.—Do you believe that the schools should give boys and girls systematic instruction in sex questions? (Phenomena of reproduction, comparative anatomy, and venereal diseases).

2.—If so, at what age do you believe instruction should be given?

3.—What methods should be employed (Lectures, illustrated by lantern slides, films, graphs, presentation of live illustrations, visits to museums, etc.)

4.—Should this instruction be for boys only or for both sexes? (Instruction of course to be in separate sessions and woman instructors for girls, men for boys).

5.—Should the instruction be entrusted to the teachers or limited to physicians? Possibly nurses? (Women physicians for girls).

6.—Should sex education be included in the regular course of instruction in the natural sciences (elementary and secondary instruction.)

7.—Should the necessary knowledge on sex subjects be added to the text books now used by pupils or in separate pamphlet form?

Note—These are the questions sent out in order to ascertain the view of the public, in anticipation of an international consideration of this subject.

Spoiling Children.

"Thou must be brave thyself
If thou the truth would teach."

and with Luther we say:

"Put thou thy trust in God
In duty's path go on."

A single virtuous action has elevated a whole city, a whole nation. No good example dies. It lives on forever in our race. Man's best products are his happy and sanctifying family. It is from small seeds dropped into the ground that the finest productions grow.

There is nothing more abhorrent than an impudent, selfish, ill-mannered child, yet is it the child's fault? We blame the little one but should not this judgment be placed on the shoulders of the parents?

Un-selfishness and complete devotion of parents to their children can take many mistaken forms. Parents deny themselves in life that the children may have. Often times this self denial begets a contemptuous attitude toward the parent by the petted one. In the family it is share and share alike and if self denial must be practiced let the children know and appreciate that it is for youth to give way to age. This precept reflects itself all through the happy home. Father likes to see mother well dressed and surely he takes pride in seeing his daughters also but if it is a choice of who is to be preferred there is no doubt but that children must subordinate themselves and their wishes to that of their mother's. Quite often the father, too, sacrificing for the appearance of his chidlren becomes habitually shabby, this may jeopardize his position, may cost him his pride and in time is more than likely to generate contempt from the children for whom he made this self-denial.

Parents, both father and mother, should make every effort to keep up with, and if possible, ahead of the children intellectually. Cultivate a good English-speaking vocabulary, so as to lead in conversation and not be submerged in modern slang and gutter talk. Charm of manner should be cultivated so as to give the growing ones something to imitate. The same is true of dress. For their own sake and the sake of the home—loved so much by all—never allow yourself in any respect, even that of dress, to be relegated to the background. This is not kindness to your children to let them have every thing, every whim or wish gratified. They must make their contribution and not have father or mother or both surrender their personalities and become mere drudges for the little ones.

Parents' preservation of their own rights of personality, for their own sake, must be done with tact, never in any spirit of temper and firmness: it all depends upon inward poise of parent, and the certainty of their place, their sympathy with life and the realization of leadership by the subordinate members of the family group.

There must be a "give-and-take" between mother and daughters, between father and sons, which, rightly maintained, gives a mutual helpfulness of the greatest value and significance. This cannot exist where position is surrendered and children are constantly allowed to have all, thereby absorbing the personalities of the devoted parents, relegating mother and father to the background at the expense of self expression and authority.

Parents who thus spoil their children develop ingrates and will live to see the day when the training of youth—or lack of it—returns to sorrow their age.

The most attractive children are those showing loving consideration and thoughtfulness to their parents, particularly when old and in need of assistance. This attractiveness is the result of training. Parents must therefore hold their places as "head of the home" and as such it will mean, even in these modern times, happiness for all.

FACTS ABOUT PARENTHOOD

Prepared by

S. DANA HUBBARD, M.D.
NEW YORK

*Attending Dermatologist to the
New York City Children's Hospital
Dermatologist Letchworth Village
Director
Bureau Public Health Education, New York City
Department of Health*

MOTHERHOOD.

"Come let us all pull together and make the path of life easy and straight for the little feet of our Children."

The one AIM of this pamphlet is to
SAVE THE BABIES.

The great responsibility of life approaches with the advent of Motherhood. This responsibility, which may be evaded many times, nevertheless must be met or nature's just debt will be paid.

Before Baby Comes.

Motherhood should cause no fear of trouble, because birth is a natural event. It is only where human beings have departed from nature to such an extent that they lead almost abnormal lives that this ordeal need be approached with misgivings and fears.

As soon as you know that a baby is to be expected—stoppage of menstruation, enlargement of breasts, morning sickness, etc.,—you should engage the best doctor you can afford and place yourself under his or her care.

If you have had one miscarriage or an abortion, another may be prevented by proper treatment.

If you cannot afford a physician, apply to a hospital or clinic where experienced doctors and nurses will advise you.

Needs of the Expectant Mother.

The expectant mother requires an extra amount of sleep, rest, food, water, and refreshment. She needs an extra amount of fresh air.

Climbing stairs, use of sewing machines, hard household or laborious factory work, in the later months of pregnancy—child carrying—should be avoided as it may tend to bring on a miscarriage or make the infant small and delicate.

Violent exercise is prohibited during this trying period.

Daily bathing is necessary for the best health of the mother.

At least one movement of the bowels daily is necessary. If this be difficult to bring about you should consult your doctor because salts may disturb the nutrition of your blood and pills may disarrange your pregnancy.

A nervous, overworked, underfed woman cannot expect to have a strong vigorous healthy child. The farmer in selecting stock for breeding, picks the best and in trying to produce the best, he cares for these parents of his coming stock as well as he knows how. Surely mankind in reproducing human beings should not do less.

When labor is threatened during the later months of pregnancy the expectant mother should go to bed at once and remain quiet until all danger be past.

Fresh air is necessary for both mother and child and therefore rest in the open air is desired. Sleeping with windows open is needed. Walking for short periods is desirable during the entire course of pregnancy. Exercise in the air is better than medicine.

To drain the poisons of the body, which gather quickly during this period, the kidneys should be well flushed. To do this satisfactorily plenty of water should be taken.

Loose comfortable clothing is essential to the comfort of the mother and the well being of the infant. All clothing should hang from the shoulders. There should be no tight bands. Round garters are bad, as they interfere with the free circulation of the blood and tend to develop enlarged veins in the legs.

The breasts and nipples should be kept clean, and especially when the breasts are pendulous, should be well powdered underneath several times a day. The skin of the nipple should be toughened and to accomplish this massage and rub with vaseline. After the bath a little alcohol in the form of "Cologne Water" may be used. Always dry well. If the skin of the nipples is well prepared nursing is a pleasure instead of a discomfort.

Growth requires food, and so expectant mothers must have plenty of simple nourishing food. The baby must not be starved before it is born. There is a tradition that if mothers eat much the baby will be large and difficulty experienced at birth. This is positively untrue. Tea and crackers will not make milk. Highly seasoned foods, rich and fried foods should be either avoided or else eaten sparingly. It is not so much what the mother eats as it is how she eats it, when she eats it and how much she takes. Be careful in your diet. Eat slowly. Chew your food well. Eat wisely. Overeating taxes the organs which take care of waste and may cause serious illness.

Signs of Pregnancy—"Being-in-a-family way".

The first and most natural question of the young woman is, "How does pregnancy manifest itself?"

The presumtive signs of pregnancy are these:—

a Cessation of menstruation.
b Changes in the breasts.
c Morning sickness.
d Disturbances in passing water (Urination).

The importance of these is in the stated order. None is positive but in group formation in a woman, otherwise well these signs are fairly positive.

Morning sickness is the occurrence of nausea, usually upon arising, with or without vomiting, and is noted in about 2/3 of the instances of pregnancy. It is as a rule most noticeable in the first pregnancy.

Difficult or painful passage of water may be an early sign and the desire to frequently pass water in order to empty the bladder is due to the enlarging womb pressing upon the bladder walls. This may disappear after several weeks as the womb rises into the abdomen and relieves this pressure.

One of the most significant of the results of pregnancy is Life. This is technically called "quickening" and is felt by the mother about the 16th or 18th week of pregnancy. After this sensation there can scarcely be any room for doubt that pregnancy exists.

Duration of Pregnancy.

From an observation of numerous cases of child birth, in many countries and under all conditions of life, the length of the period of human gestation —carrying-the-child—has come to be regarded as approximately 39 weeks or 273 days. Counting 30 days to the month it will be seen that the commonly accepted period of "Nine months" is nearly correct.

To estimate the date of an expected normal birth physicians employ a rule, which while not exact, gives a close reckoning. This method consists in counting forward 280 days from the beginning of the last menstrual period. The simplest method however is to count backward 3 months and add 7 days from the first day of the last period. Example, if the last menstruation was October 30, count back 3 months, this is July 30, add 7 days gives August 6 as the presumptive approximate date. About once in twenty times the date is exact. Otherwise it may be a few days ahead or several later but that is about as near the period as it can be definitely determined.

Care of the Mother's Teeth.

The teeth are thought to be more susceptible to decay during pregnancy than ordinarily. This may be partly explained by the demand for the lime salts needed to build up the child's bony frame and partly by the effect that the regurgitated stomach contents, which are strongly acid, may play in the development and enlargement of cavities of decay in the mother's teeth.

For these reasons hygiene of the mouth is most important during this period.

As soon as the woman knows that she is pregnant she should go to a good dentist and have such repairs made to her teeth as may be needed. This can have a beneficial effect only when attended to at an early period.

The teeth should be brushed and cleaned carefully after each meal, and the mouth carefully rinsed after any attack of vomiting or gas eructation. There are numerous excellent mouth washes but a teaspoonful of milk of magnesia or a tablespoonful of lime water in a glass of moderately warm water makes an excellent antiseptic mouth wash.

The Complications of Pregnancy.

Constipation, piles, and indigestion. These may occur at irregular intervals but when annoying consult your medical adviser.

Nausea and vomiting are to be expected but they may assume an abnormal severity and medical care is essential to control them.

Heartburn is the sensation of a 'burning in the throat' and is incident to the abnormal development of acid in the stomach. This may be relieved by warm milk, or soda in solution or olive oil twenty minutes before meal time. Eliminating all fats may also help but if home remedies fail, then seek medical advice.

Disturbances of the kidneys are common and often serious. Take no chances, have the water examined periodically and if the urine is concentrated as shown by high color and heavy sediment drink more water or consult your doctor.'

Cramps especially in the lower limbs due to pressure on the nerves are very uncomfortable and may occur on awakening, especially during endeavors to stretch. This pain may be relieved by relaxing and rubbing the limb or applying hot cloths and elevating the feet.

Swollen veins (varicose veins) are due to undue pressure and are a rather general accomplishment of pregnancy. This means that the patient must rest and sit about with feet more or less elevated. Relief may be afforded by bandaging—strips of wool 2 or 3 inches wide wound about the leg like a soldier's puttee from the ankle up—never from above downward.

"Whites"—Leucorrhoea—a whitish discharge from the vagina, due to the congestion of the vaginal walls, resulting from pressure of the enlarging uterus (womb) is often annoying but rarely serious. Douches should not be taken except under medical advice.

Toxemia—Poisoning of Pregnancy.

As a child in the uterus grows there is constantly sent back to the mother's blood an increasing amount of waste material and if, in addition the mother's own nutritional processes are imperfect or her organs of excretion are not functioning normally, there is difficulty in eliminating this waste which may result seriously for either mother or child or both. This condition is known as "toxemia."

Some of the common symptoms of this condition are:—

1. Persistent or serious vomiting.
2. Repeated headaches.
3. Dizziness.
4. Puffiness about the face and hands.
5. Spots before the eyes—blurring of vision.
6. Muscular twitching—simulating convulsions.
7. Neuralgic pains.

One or more of these unpleasant symptoms do not necessarily signify this unpleasant condition but when they do occur it is well to seek medical care promptly. There is no truth in the old adage of the home that "a sick pregnancy is a safe one". On the other hand many a precious mother's life has been sacrificed by believing in these superstitious old sayings.

There is no virtue—either in pregnancy or in any other condition—in enduring any pain or distress that can be prevented by proper means and much harm may result from neglect to secure suitable medical advice promptly.

Every pregnant woman must strive to keep in mind plain and simple rules for health and obey them unreservedly.

Mother's Mark. Maternal Impressions.

By a 'maternal impression' is meant an injurious physical modification of the child through the influence of some harmful state of mind of the mother.

There is current more MISINFORMATION on this matter than on any other subject and it would seem fitting that it be given careful consideration.

There is a well established and age old impression that 'marking' of babies is possible by maternal impression. It will comfort the more intelligent women to know on what a slight and uncertain foundation this belief rests. Doctors are agreed most happily for all these opinions of maternal impressions have no basis in fact.

1. There is no connection between the mother and the child in the uterus by which nerve or thought impressions can be conveyed. In fact, it appears from anatomical studies, that nature has erected a positive barrier especially for the protection of the infant from such injuries.

2. There are few mothers who have not at some time during the carrying of the child had experiences of a disturbing nature of greater or less severity. Accordingly most babies ought, to be born marked if the belief holds true.' This is not the case. It has not been the case, even when such a result was expected. When one thinks of the many strange and unhappy things that daily

occur it is not remarkable that pregnant women should encounter them sufficiently often to bring about many odd and striking coincidences.

3. Many women do not realize that they are pregnant until about the 6 or 8 week and do not begin to worry about the baneful effects of which they hear until pregnancy is well advanced.

The mother is not a passive instrument in the process of embryonic development. The harm which a mother may pass to her fetal child is not the physical marking but through improper ordering of her own life, she may disorder the child's future happiness by giving it an impaired constitution. The child is protected from direct injury but the child is dependent upon the mother for the materials of nutrition and it is only through nutrition that the mother can influence the growth of the child.

Should a mother not live a well regulated and ordered life during her pregnancy, should she pine and lament it is conceivable that the child will be robbed of the nutrition needed for development.

There can be little doubt that many puny, unhealthy youngsters, wailing sickly crying children, did not get their right sort of nutrition during the pre-birth period and that their nervous condition may be attributed by their mothers to maternal impressions. Scientifically the reason is a deeper one than impression — it was a physical deprivation and doubtless the death of many babies may be traceable to such causes.

Away with the bogey—there is no such thing as a mother's mark. Maternal impressions having physical harmful influence exist in the minds of uninformed ignorant individuals and such beliefs cannot be demonstrated scientifically.

What to prepare. Necessary Things for the Baby.

Light weight flannel ¾ yard of thin pure wool.

Two light weight woolen blankets.

Three cotton and wool undershirts.

Three flannel skirts.

Three Outing flannel gowns.

Four cotton slips.

1½ dozen diapers 18 inches.

1½ dozen diapers 22 inches.

One pound of Powdered Boric Acid.

One Box Talcum Powder.

Several pieces of Castile Soap—white for infant, colored for mother. The colors do not mean any difference in the quality of the soap but the soap for the infant should not be used by the mother and vice versa.

¼ lb. sterile gauze.

¼ pound sterile absorbent cotton.

Two dozen safety pins—large and small.

One set of baby scales—spring balance.

Necessary Things for the Mother.

Three Night gowns

A head cap.

1½ yards square of rubber sheeting.

Two pounds of absorbent cotton.

One ounce of Vaseline.

Two pounds of sterile gauze.

One rubber douche bag and glass nozzle.

One metal douche pan.

One metal bed pan.

One metalwash—hand—basin.

These are the minimum necessary materials for

a clean home confinement. The surgeon will furnish instruments and materials for 'drops' for babies eyes, for tying cord, for sewing tears, and the necessary disinfectants for hands and skin.

The New Born.

There should be a warm soft blanket to receive the child immediately after birth, the child should be oiled and not immediately bathed.

There should be special consideration given the eyes of the newborn, a two per cent nitrate of silver solution 3 drops instilled at once into each eye by the doctor or the nurse. After a little time wash the eyes with a saturated boric acid solution. This may prevent sore eyes and possibly blindness.

The baby, eyes cleansed, oiled, and wrapped in warm blanket should be placed in a warm bassinet or basket or box and kept warm. It has been living at a temperature of 98 degrees and to prevent exposure to the temperature of the ordinary room giving a chill and making the baby sick it should be permitted to get accustomed to its new surroundings. A cold gives a young baby snuffles and these choke its breathing apparatus and kill it quickly.

The baby's eyes are also unaccustomed to the light of day and here additional protection must be given. Keep the eyes shaded for a day or two and never allow sunlight to shine or the room light to glare directly into the baby's face.

After the oil has soaked in and the mother has been given the necessary attention the nurse is free to bathe the baby and dress it.

Reasons why a mother should nurse her baby.

Breast Milk is always ready and is never sour.

Breast milk does not have to be prepared or measured.

Breast milk is nature's method and was intended for the baby.

Breast milk will make the baby strong and healthy.

Breast milk is free from dirt, germs, and the flies cannot get at it.

Breast milk protects your baby from many infants' diseases.

Breast fed babies are healthiest. One breast fed baby dies to ten bottle fed. Give your baby the advantage of these long odds in its fight for life.

Breast milk is the only perfect food for the baby.

Breast fed babies seldom have bowel trouble which is so fatal in bottle fed babies, especially during the hot weather.

Your baby will have the best chance of living and thriving if it is breast fed.

Nursing.

There are no particular rules for this form of diet. Each baby is a rule unto itself. There are some general rules for guidance but none for strict acceptance.

The baby should not be put to the breast for 5 or 6 hours after birth.

During the first 24 hours the baby should not nurse more than 4 times, but both breasts each time. If the infant cries much, boiled and cooled water—unsweetened—should be given. It is the custom of some lazy folks to feed the infant at this time sweetened water or weak tea, but this is wrong. It starts bowel trouble because the infant cannot digest the sugar though it tastes good and is acceptable.

Beginning with the third day, when the mother begins to give milk, nurse the baby every three hours, alternating the breasts, or taking both breasts each time according to the appetite and amount of milk secreted. Never let the baby remain at the breast for a longer period than twenty minutes in all.

Nursing time should be regulated by the clock. Regular feeding means regular sleep and these things make the care of the baby much easier and gives the mother time for rest and comfort.

In the beginning, to form good habits it is well to wake the baby at nursing time: soon the habit will be formed and the baby will awaken at the regular interval.

Training is tedious and difficult but perseverance and patience are required and if persisted in will succeed. But few people have the necessary patience or fortitude to properly train babies and that is one of the reasons for much of the unhappiness of homes.

In case the milk is delayed beyond the third day, the baby should be fed at regular three hour intervals, but before artificial feeding is used put the infant to the breast in order to stimulate the flow of milk.

Hours for Nursing.

Until baby is 4 months old nurse every three hours up to ten o'clock at night and only once during the night: seven nursings in the 24 hours time.

After 4 months of age, omit all night nursings. Give six nursings in twenty-four hours.

When 6 months old nurse every 4 hours—usually giving both breasts each time—only five nursings each 24 hours.

Should the baby cry between feedings, give cooled boiled water without anything in it.

Never forget to give the baby cooled boiled water regularly. This is frequently overlooked and time and again restless crying babies have been quieted by simply slackening their thirst. Once the writer was called after midnight to a young family for a restless crying child. On careful examination nothing wrong was discovered so he gave the infant a drink and it immediately went to sleep much to the discomfiture of the uninformed parents. Never forget a baby gets thirsty.

Do not wean or give other feeding without medical advice.

Never indefinitely nurse a baby. When teeth appear it is approaching weaning time.

Never use a sucking teat or pacifier. It is unnecessary and is harmful as it may excite gas in the stomach and deform the teeth. Once the habit is acquired, it is difficult to break up.

Weaning Baby.

There are times when the baby should be weaned.

If the mother becomes ill of any serious or acute disease the baby should be weaned.

Unless specially indicated weaning should be under a doctor's instructions.

If baby is thriving, the time for weaning varies between 6 and 10 months of age.

•Weaning should be a gradual process, if possible, by giving the baby at first one, later two or more feedings from a cup or bottle in place of nursing. Then increase the feedings and diminish the breast nursings until discontinuance is possible without the child's notice.

If baby is weaned before 8 months it should be taught to take the bottle—if at ten or eleven months old, it is better to teach it to drink or feed from the spoon.

If at all possible to avoid it, never wean in the summer months.

Things which are bad for all babies.

Thumb Sucking, Pacifiers, Soothing Syrups—facetiously styled "Baby Killers". 'Patent' medicines. Colic remedies of gin or whiskey.

Dirty play things, dirty nipples, dirty bottles, dirty floors.

Rubber or waterproof diapers—except for very temporary use.

Moving picture shows.

Violent rocking, shaking up, bouncing, screaming near face or ears.

Play after feeding.

Kissing baby in the mouth—either by home folks or by others.

Never permit any one to kiss a baby in its mouth. Diphtheria, Whooping cough and other serious sickness is communicated by this disgusting and most pernicious practice. An infant should be permitted to go through at least its first year with out contracting any illness. If it does not, then carelessness of the known rules of hygiene has caused this and the illness is retribution for such carelessness.

Never test the temperature of the baby's milk by taking the nipple in your mouth. Never permit a nurse or other attendant to do this. Use a thermometer or feel it with the back of the hand.

Never let a baby suck on an empty bottle.

Do not permit sleeping on the mother's breast while nursing.

Sleeping in bed with the mother is dangerous as a number of distressing accidents fatal to the infant have occurred from neglecting this precaution.

Spitting or wiping with a mouth wetted handkerchief to clean baby's face.

Sneezing or coughing in the baby's face.

Allowing a person with a cough or cold to hold the baby.

Allowing any person with consumption (tuberculosis) to take care of the baby. Have your nurses carefully examined by your family physician. Let him exclude tuberculosis and syphilis from your nurse.

"Baby is not a toy, neither is it a plaything. A baby is a great responsibility. Baby's health, growth, development, and future happiness depends upon father and mother. Mostly on mother.

Bottle Feeding. Artificial Feeding.

There is no perfect substitute for breast milk. The best advice here is DON'T.

Clean, fresh cow's milk properly altered (modified) is the best substitute available, though goats milk answers nicely and is usually well borne by the baby.

Patent foods—unless specially prescribed by your medical adviser should be avoided. They are not fresh, they are expensive, and babies fed upon them are more liable to be sick than those fed on cow's milk.

Care of baby's Milk.

Buy the best milk you can afford, its price may seem high but in the end it is the cheapest.

Buy only selected bottled milk from a clean certified dairy, and keep the milk and its containers clean in your home.

Milk is easily spoiled, a fly dropping into the milk is sufficient to spoil the whole bottle.

Buy the freshest milk you can get, but not the richest.

Don't take a chance with old or stale milk.

Dipped, loose milk is never clean and its never safe for baby feeding. Only milk in bottles should be used to feed the baby.

When received the milk bottle should be immediately washed off and at once placed on ice and kept there. Warm milk spoils readily and spoiled milk will make the baby sick. Never use milk for feeding baby that has been standing in the sun or which has been left exposed uncovered.

Never buy milk from the milkman by leaving a pitcher out of doors for milkman to fill. It is exposed to dust and dirt and insects which may breed disease.

Not only bottles, dishes, and ice box should be kept clean but the hands of every one handling baby's milk should be clean and especially cleaned before preparing the milk for feeding.

New rubber nipples should be turned inside out and boiled.

All nipples after using should be carefully washed in soap and water and kept in water in a glass with some boric acid and covered. **Always** rinse before using.

Modifying and preparing baby's food.

The simplest plan of modifying is to take whole milk—from a bottle well shaken up—and dilute according to child's age and digestion.

Beginning on the third day, the average baby should be given 3 ounces of milk daily diluted with 7 ounces of sterile water; to this mixture add one tablespoon of lime water and two level teaspoons of cane sugar. This is sufficient for 7 feedings. Sterile water is made of boiling water and letting cool and store in a well corked clean bottle. Lime water is best purchased at the drug store. Use granulated sugar, never powdered or confectioner's or glucose sugars.

At 7 days of age, the average infant requires about 5 ounces of milk daily, which may be diluted with 10 ounces of water and to this mixture add one and a half teaspoons of sugar and 1 ounce of lime water, this amount being sufficient for 7 feedings.

The milk should be increased by one-half ounce every 4 days.

The water should be increased by one-half ounce every 8 days.

Feedings at three months of age.

The average child requires 16 ounces of milk daily diluted with an equal amount of water, to this should be added 3 tablespoons of sugar and 2 ounces of lime water. This amount should be divided into 6 feedings.

The milk should be increased by one-half ounce about every 6 days.

The water should be REDUCED by one-half ounce every two weeks.

At the sixth month, the average child requires 24 ounces of milk daily, which should be diluted with 12 ounces of water, to which is added 3 even tablespoons of sugar and two ounces of lime water. This should be divided into 5 feedings.

The amount of milk should be increased by one-half ounce weekly.

The milk should be increased only if the baby is hungry and is digesting its food well. It should not be increased unless there is hunger for more food, nor if the baby is suffering from indigestion even though the infant appears to be hungry.

At nine months of age—The average child requires 30 ounces of milk daily which should be diluted with 10 ounces of water, to which is added two even tablespoons of sugar and two ounces of lime water. This amount being divided into 5 feedings.

The sugar added may be milk sugar or if unobtainable, there may be substituted granulated cane sugar, or maltose—malt sugar.

Facts about Water for Baby.

At first plain sterile water should be used to dilute the milk. At three months, some times earlier, a weak barley water may be used in lieu of the plain water.

Barley water is made by taking one-half tablespoon (level) of barley flour to 16 ounces of water and cook for twenty minutes.

Between feedings give the baby water from a clean spoon.

At six months of age, the barley flour may be increased to one and a half even tablespoons cooked in 12 ounces of water for twenty minutes.

At nine months, the barley flour may be increased to 3 level tablespoons, cooked in 8 ounces of water for twenty minutes.

These feedings for the average are for general guides.

Each infant is a rule unto itself. A large baby may require additions to these average amounts while a tiny puny or small baby may require a reduction in the amounts.

All rules for bottle feeding should be strictly carried out and never departed from once you have struck the right ration.

Regularity is of the utmost importance. Nothing so upsets an infant as irregular feeding in varying amounts with varying materials. Exactness is the price of health.

If a child does not take all of the feeding throw out the remaining part. Never warm over again for a later feeding.

Unless a baby has loose bowel movements it should be given from one to three tablespoons of strained fruit juice (Orange) once daily after 7 or 8 months of age.

After nine months of age give squeezed beef juice, beef tea, or plain mutton or chicken broth once a day.

When ten months old the baby may be given a part of a soft egg, a small piece of crisp toast or sweiback or a crust of bread to chew immediately after the feeding.

Other solid foods should not be given during the first year.

Never give a baby ice cream, ice cream soda or

ice cream cones. Never let a baby suck on a loly-
pop.

At one year of age the baby may take milk un-
diluted and a strained cereal in addition may be
given once or twice a day.

Changing Baby's food from Bottle to Table Food.

During the second year of life, the baby should
have four meals a day—8 A.M., 11 A. M., 2 P. M.,
and about 6 P. M., and nothing but water allowed
between meals.

At 12 months of age the baby should be weaned
from the bottle and taught to drink from a cup.

When weaning from bottle the baby may have
4 cups of milk a day.

At about 15 or 16 months of age, the baby may
have a teaspoon of scraped rare beef, mutton or
chicken.

At about 18 months of age there may be given
one-half of a mashed mealy baked white potato
daily.

When two years of age there may be given green
vegetables preferably the fresh ones, only when
thoroughly cooked and finely washed.

Tea, coffee, wine, cider, beer, soda water, co-
coa, and candy should never be given to a young
infant.

The juices of fresh fruits may be given after
12 months of age. Cooked fruit, such as baked ap-
ple, or applesauce, should be given once a day
after the child is 18 months old. This at first
should be carefully strained to free the pulp of
seeds, fible, or skins.

Over ripe, stale raw fruits are dangerous, especially in summer and in the city.

General Care of Baby.

Clothing in summer should be light and on very hot days only a napkin should be worn.

Bathe the baby morning and evening and on hot days in the middle of the day.

Always keep the skin of the baby clean and well powdered.

Napkins when wet or soiled should at once be placed in water and washed as soon as possible.

The baby needs an abundance of fresh air. Keep out of doors as much as possible. Avoid the sun on hot days. In very hot days take baby out in the early morning and in the late afternoon and early evening. It is often cooler in the house with the shutters closed in the middle of the day in summer time.

Take the baby to the park, to the beaches, and to the country when ever it is possible. The baby will enjoy riding and motoring. When riding protect from draught.

Protect the baby from mosquitoes.

Place of Confinement.

This is a question of money, choice, and fashion.

It is becoming more and more common for women to go to a hospital to be confined. This has a great many advantages. It is cheaper, safer, and many times more convenient than being confined at home. In an emergency there are always experienced doctors and nurses at hand and if additional help is needed during such stresses it may also be quickly obtained. In fact hospital selection for confinement has so many advantages over being confined at home that a comparison is well nigh impossible.

If a confinement is at home, arrangements

should be made for medical care and for nurses' attendance well in advance and also terms agreed upon in order to avoid disturbing and annoying argument during a period when such business transactions upset and may be followed by more or less serious consequences.

If the confinement is a normal one, and by vast numbers the majority, there should be some one in the house to do the house work while the mother is confined to her bed. The needs of the mother and baby are first consideration but some one has got to be able to prepare meals, clean clothing and keep house while the little house keeper is away from her post. The best nursing is necessary for mother and child during this period and no pains should be spared to get the best and most experienced.

In the care of the baby the following list will be found convenient.

A baby bath tub of galvanized iron.

Drying frames for clothing.

Apron of turkish toweling or outing flannel.

A low rocker preferably one without arms.

Baby scales.

A low screen to keep wind off baby when being bathed.

A low table—a small kitchen table with legs sawed off—on which to dress and undress baby and hold tub in case a standing up position is desired.

A baby's diary—or book of principal events.

For a Nursing Mother.

The diet for a nursing mother, is usually that for the mother during pregnancy. It should be laxative, nutritious and above all appetizing.

The mother may be permitted to follow her own wishes as to the choice of her food in most instances.

The old idea that acid fruits and vegetables gave baby cholic is probably not true. However if on experience it is found that certain foods or drink disturb the mother's digestion this naturally will have an unpleasant or unfavorable effect upon the milk. It is therefore necessary to watch the diet carefully.

Advise the mother to eat slowly, to chew her food carefully and above all to refrain from worry or excitement. Constipation should be guarded against as carefully during lactation as during pregnancy.

If milk is scanty, the need for more generous diet is indicated. Plenty of fresh milk, eggs, fresh vegetables, ripe fruit, and any plain simple well balanced food is required.

If the appetite is capricious, it is well to eat lightly 5 or 6 light meals a day.

A quiet state of mind is essential for all nursing mothers, and this matter cannot be given too much importance. Nothing will interfere so completely with the secretion of milk as an over-wrought nervous condition. Every thought must be given that it is for the sake of the life of the child.

Surround the mother with things that interest her. She is entitled now to all the pleasures possible. Out door life is especially indicated. The mother should try to get 8 hours sleep daily. Plenty of sunshine is highly desirable.

When the doctor's visits become irregular, and the nurse goes, the mother is likely to become nervous and discouraged and her milk supply becomes lessened. She is likely to think that she is starving the baby and give up nursing but this is a great mistake.

The strain at this period is great but it gets less and less day by day and as mother and baby become adjusted to the new conditions, the health of both improves and the lost spirits revive and health becomes normal. With this the milk comes more freely.

If the mother will have courage and patience and will strive to carry herself and her baby past this epoch she will in all likelihood be well able to nurse to the end quite successfully. At least every possible means to this end should be tried before any change is contemplated or made.

The return of the menstrual period is not a sufficient reason for weaning, but the occurence of a new pregnancy demands weaning, as the mother's strength will hardly be sufficient for this additional burden. If at all possible it is wise to prevent conception during the nursing period of the new born. Regarding this your physician should advise you.

See that the baby's birth is reported. It may be of importance some time to have an official record of this birth. It would be well to have your names ready for the baby on arrival—make two selections, two names for a girl and two names for a boy and settle upon a selection that a public record may at once be made. The law requires the physician under penalty to report the birth within a week, in some communities within ten days.

Whipping?

Whipping may in some instances be necessary. But I am unalterably opposed to corporal punishment. If I had to admit myself worsted by a child and had to resort to force to have my child obey me I would feel that I was unsuited for parenthood. As a father of two girls raised in a large congested city I am proud to say that I have never had to think of much less threaten to punish by flogging. My girls are grown and two happier and better disciplined children I do not know.

Truthfulness and lying are opposites in human nature. It is necessary to prove to a child the reasons for honesty and the uselessness of the other. I would that my parents had been as particular. It may be with some natures that honesty is innate but it is the most difficult thing in life to implant. By nature we desire and it is natural to acquire. It is by culture that this desire is directed along proper channels so that we may acquire in the ways in which no harm or injury is done to another. This is education. It is that form of education that has to be started early and implanted in the little mind until it is literally second nature.

Never underestimate your own ability. The average adult knows sufficient to satisfy the child. It is not necessary to go into minute details of explanation but an answer that is truthful and pointed can always be given. The mind of the child if it is inclined to ask embarrassing questions can be easily diverted by springing a new subject. A horse will shy and if shying is to be encouraged, then hurt or frighten the animal when employing this bad habit. But if it is decided to break up this practice, divert the animal's attention.

, Manners are an artificial acquirement and every child must be taught. At home the manners of the family are quickly indicated by the child's behavior. Public manners should be taught by outside teachers, preferably dancing school or physical training classes. The trained child stands out in a group like a thoroughbred does among a bunch of runts. Manners make the man and the lady.

If you have a daughter think of the following:

Try to make the girls feel that mother loves them and that nothing which happens in their daily lives is too small to interest mother.

The big thing in the companionship of your own girl is to show them that mother has compassion and love and understanding.

Three fourths of the girls who go astray do so because they have no one to go and appeal to in time of trial, who will give advice and not criticism. Parents scold children away from them.

A girl's self-respect should never be jeopardized.

There is joy and hope for the girl in the happy companionable home, but the home is useless to the girl unless she is understood.

Girls have three ages; Chronological, Biological, Psychological. Each age must be anticipated and the girl prepared accordingly.

That the majority of girls who leave home or go astray are feeble-minded or mentally deranged is a mistaken notion.

The feeble minded girl lacks cleverness and wit. She is mentally heavy and simple minded.

The big thing in this training of girls is to have

patience with the child. Punishment is not always necessary to correct misbehavior. Read in another pamphlet about the unadjusted girl, the misfit and the working girl.

Invite the confidence of your girls, remove fears of censure, punishment and criticism. If the child knows she will be given a fair open unbiased hearing the spirit of repentance and willingness to do right for right's sake can be easily aroused. This is the highest way of dealing with behavior in our estimation.

The boys' problem is dealt with under "Messages."

EDITORS' ACKNOWLEDGMENTS

We would like to thank our editor, Peter Hubbard, for having the idea for this project and the sense of humor and intellect to make it happen. As before, his skill makes us look a whole lot better. Thanks as well to production editor Mary Beth Constant and the rest of the terrific team at HarperCollins.

Dr. S. Dana Hubbard, whether or not you threw "light where shadows fall," who can say? But you surely tried, and for that we are extremely grateful.